THE **LOVE WINS** COMPANION

THE **LOVE WINS** COMPANION

A Study Guide for Those Who Want to Go Deeper

ROB BELL

EDITED BY DAVID VANDERVEEN

HarperOne
An Imprint of HarperCollins*Publishers*

Permissions can be found on page 197.

Unless otherwise noted, all biblical quotations are taken from the Holy Bible, Today's New International Version®. Copyright © 2001, 2005 by Biblica®. Used by permission of Biblica®. All rights reserved worldwide.

HarperCollins books may be purchased for educational, business, or sales promotional use. For information please write: Special Markets Department, HarperCollins Publishers, 10 East 53rd Street, New York, NY 10022.

HarperCollins website: http://www.harpercollins.com

HarperCollins®, ®, and HarperOne™
are trademarks of HarperCollins. Publishers.

FIRST EDITION

Library of Congress Cataloging-in-Publication Data is available upon request.

ISBN 978-0-06-212280-3

11 12 13 14 15 RRD(H) 10 9 8 7 6 5 4 3 2 1

CONTENTS

FOREWORD

DO NOT BE AFRAID

BY JACK HEASLIP

Do you know how many times the phrase "Do not be afraid" appears in the Bible? One website says it is 365 times. I prefer to say "lots of times."

What has fear to do with a book on love? God's love at that? Even before *Love Wins* was released, fear was at work. People had opinions about a book they hadn't read. I was told I needed to be skeptical, suspicious, nervous, critical, afraid, but mostly "cautious." Caution must be good, mustn't it? The trouble is that caution can be fear dressed up to look right and proper and maybe a shade holy.

Fear also could be heard in the questions being asked. Is it okay to question God like that? Is he destroying faith? Why doesn't he respect our tradition, our catechism?

If you are in a group, look around and see how many people show signs of fear and suspicion. Look in a mirror for the same signs.

Jesus said, "Do not be afraid." Angels said, "Do not be afraid." God said it too.

> After all these things, this word of God came to Abram in a vision: "Don't be afraid, Abram. I'm your shield. Your reward will be grand." (Gen. 15:1, MSG)
>
> But the angel assured her, "Mary, you have nothing to fear. God has a surprise for you." (Luke 1:30, MSG)
>
> But Jesus was quick to comfort them. "Courage, it's me. Don't be afraid." (Matt. 14:27, MSG)

So why shouldn't we be afraid? Because God can be trusted.

So with a God who can be trusted we can head off into new territory or a fresh experience of old territory. We can ask questions. We do not need to be afraid.

Because we can trust God and not be afraid, we are then free to love. Love is the bottom line!

> Everyone who loves is born of God and experiences a relationship with God. (1 John 4:7, MSG)

It is like love meeting love. Our shallow attempts at loving are embraced by God's mighty love. That, for me, is powerful stuff. With that sort of confidence we can really go for the experience and the understanding of God.

> There is no room in love for fear. Well-formed love banishes fear. Since fear is crippling, a fearful life—

> fear of death, fear of judgment—is one not yet fully formed in love. (1 John 4:18, MSG)

God is love! It's that simple, that profound.

Paul believed this. He gave the Corinthians a wonderful description of what our religion should involve and what it should look like: "For in Christ, neither our most conscientious religion nor disregard of religion amounts to anything. What matters is something far more interior: faith expressed in love" (Gal. 5:6, MSG).

Isn't that brilliant? Religion and nonreligion are firmly put in their place by God's love. And our intellects are given something to work on. Paul encourages us to think! It is okay to think! Sometimes our little gray cells are put on the back burner by those who want us to follow a faith they prescribe. It is good to unwrap a package. How can we receive the gift if we don't delve a bit?

Do not be afraid. God can be trusted. You are free to love, to explore, to ask questions, to think. That is the invitation Rob Bell puts before us in *Love Wins* and now in *The Love Wins Companion.* We are invited to step outside of the boat and draw closer to the one who calls us and wants to be known. Do not be afraid. God appreciates our efforts and smiles at our failings. He loves our humor when we lighten our load and when we enjoy the presence of his Spirit in our lives. God is willing to be found—by anyone who is looking. That's good news. And the password is *love.*

PREFACE

BY ROB BELL

I'm thrilled that you are interested in going deeper into the ideas I present in *Love Wins*. A couple of thoughts before we get going.

First, some words out there in our culture have incredibly heavy emotional attachments to them, words like *heaven, hell, judgment, salvation.* You throw these words into a conversation, and people have strong opinions and ideas whether for or against, negative or positive. This is true especially when it comes to the Christian faith, and specifically when it comes to where people are with God, who has a relationship with God, who doesn't, who's a Christian, who's not, who's going to heaven, who's going to hell.

One of the things that drives this book is my desire to simply say, "Here's what the Bible says." If some people are really, really passionate about a particular perspective, I want to know where they got that from. So when it comes to heaven and hell and judgment, what I've tried to do in the book is lay out what the Bible actually says, what Jesus said, and then, conversely, what Jesus *didn't* say.

I believe that God loves everybody. And I believe that the heart of the Christian faith is this God who loves everybody, this Jesus who came to show us this love, give us this love, and invite us into this love. So, from my perspective, the Christian faith at its core is an experience of the love of God through this Jesus, who insists that God loves everybody, everywhere. As you read through this *Companion,* as you wrestle with the questions and go further into the ideas, as you look at this passage and that passage and that story, and as you recount your own experience or reflections, my wish is to create the space where you can meet this God and experience this God's love.

I'm fascinated when Jesus talks about how he's water. It's hard to build a systematic theology around water. Try building a denomination around water; it's very fuzzy and nebulous and ambiguous—unless, of course, you're thirsty. Then you know exactly what the water is.

Or when Jesus says he's light. Light can be hard to get your hands around; it can be hard to quantify or systematize—unless you know you're far from home, and then light shows you how to return to the place from which you came.

Jesus speaks in metaphors and parables, because ultimately he comes to bring us a living, breathing experience of the love of God right here, right now. At the heart of this book is this simple, beautiful, compelling declaration that this love wins. So I hope this guide helps take you to places you haven't been before, places that are thrilling and convicting, that fill you with wonder and awe. May the peace of God be with you the whole way.

When my publisher shared with me the idea for this companion guide and asked if I could suggest who should help put it together, my first thought was my friend of twenty years Dave Vanderveen. I was of course thrilled when he said he'd do it and then continually surprised with the fresh insights and people and ideas he has brought to this project.

We have found that a lot of people are preoccupied with the question, "Is there life after death?" That's a good question, an interesting question, and one that has received a good deal of speculation and discussion. But that isn't the question that Jesus came to answer.

He came to answer a better, more urgent, more pressing question: "Is there life before death?"

And to this question Jesus repeatedly, emphatically answered, "Yes!"

That insistence of Jesus—that we can have full, overflowing, vibrant, pulsating, dynamic life right now—is what *Love Wins* is about and it's what this companion guide is about.

What's possible right now?

What is God doing in the world right here in our midst?

What does the resurrection life Jesus gives us look like at this moment in time?

My hope is that as you discuss *Love Wins* you will find yourself returning to that question and that insistence over and over and over again. My prayer is that you are not sidetracked for any significant amount of time with questions that we cannot answer, because we are speculating about things that haven't happened. My desire is that the book and now this companion will produce a profound sense of urgency and immediacy that there really is bread for the hungry and water for the thirsty and light for those who need to find their way home.

So here's to the discussion.

Enjoy.

And now, a word from Dave.

HOW TO USE THIS COMPANION

BY DAVID VANDERVEEN

Some of the Pharisees said, "Obviously, this man can't be from God. He doesn't keep the Sabbath." . . .

The man replied, "This is amazing! You claim to know nothing about him, but the fact is, he opened my eyes! It's well known that God isn't at the beck and call of sinners, but listens carefully to anyone who lives in reverence and does his will. That someone opened the eyes of a man born blind has never been heard of—ever. If this man didn't come from God, he wouldn't be able to do anything." . . .

Jesus then said, "I came into the world to bring everything into the clear light of day, making all the distinctions clear, so that those who have

> never seen will see, and those who have made a great pretense of seeing will be exposed as blind." (John 9:16, 30–33, 39, MSG)

When the blind are being healed, arguments about keeping the Sabbath seem absurd. They miss the point entirely. Jesus's words are clear about those who cannot see the light, who refuse to look away from their own interests and their own doctrines when the good news shows itself in surprising ways among us.

We all wear filters, lenses, and, in some cases, blinders when we read the Bible. No one experiences the gospel message in a vacuum. When a book appears that generates dramatic and enthusiastic interest about the underlying truth of the good news of Jesus, it demands our attention. We need to make sure we are not like those pretending to see, but are actually blind. Being open to investigating and exploring what is before us helps prevent blindness.

The problem many of us face is how to really listen—particularly as we become more comfortable with the patterns and boundaries through which we interpret the world around us. Are we truly open to God's surprises? Will we let God confront us in gut-wrenching ways with his good news? Will we let God break through our own ideas about who God is and to speak to us in fresh ways?

The most important thing for reading *Love Wins* and *The Love Wins Companion* isn't discovering the "right" beliefs about Christianity or salvation. The important thing is seriously to engage the material in the books, really attempt to read them without running the ideas through the blinders you may have, before trying to discern what the Holy Spirit may be saying through these words. Those blinders might have come from a specific Christian tradition or from another faith or no faith, whether you call yourself a believer, agnostic, atheist, or just someone looking for ideas. Dive into *Love Wins* and look around. Engage the ideas and voices in *The Love Wins Companion.* They are for those who wish to see.

We recognize that people will have different purposes for reading this companion to *Love Wins*. Some will want to explore more deeply the ideas in *Love Wins* as individuals; some will want to do the same in a small group or even in a class. We have tried to make this as open-ended and flexible as possible for all these uses. Each chapter from the original book has a corresponding section in this companion that includes an overview and introduction by Rob Bell; a general introduction of the new material by me; Bible studies and exercises for study; discussion questions for groups; and, finally, related "readings" of articles, blogs, book excerpts, and interviews to explore more deeply the ideas from the original chapter.

To get the most out of this companion, we recommend following these principles to avoid "blindness" or unnecessary division:

1. *Don't be overly focused on ending up with the right answer.* This worry often hinders our ability to hear the real question and wrestle with the issues. Relax, drop your preconceived objections, and try to re-

spond directly just to the text in front of you. The goal of both books is for you to understand what the Bible actually teaches. In the end, you might not agree with everything these books say, but we want to make sure you truly hear the questions and ideas first in case God has something new to say to you.

2. *Focus on loving the people you are discussing these issues with*—regardless of their opinion or yours. This is the explicit teaching of scripture. "No matter what I say, what I believe, and what I do, I'm bankrupt without love" (1 Cor. 13:3, MSG).
3. *Recognize that we all read the Bible through a lens and not in a vacuum.* No one "just reads the Bible." The church has been wrestling with these texts for two thousand years. There are dozens of major traditions and hundreds of minor ones that all read the biblical texts in certain ways. We are not saying the Bible is unclear or impossible to understand. But we are saying that you have filters that shape how you are reading the Bible. If you haven't identified your lenses and filters, take some time to understand your own background, biases, and the history of the ideas that have shaped your own thought.
4. *Make sure you distinguish ideas from the people who are expressing those ideas* (including your own). Candid and strong discussion is powerful and beneficial when we don't attack the people we are talking with. Debate the worthiness of the idea without infringing on the worth of the person.

5. *Make peace with the reality that good Christians can disagree on important matters.* This is another reason why it is important to separate critical comments about ideas from critical comments about people. Very bright and very devout people have a vast range of orthodox opinions that don't always align.
6. *Study the history of the idea you are defending.* Many people are shocked to discover that what they thought was ancient Christian orthodoxy turns out to be a relatively recent development in the church or, conversely, what they considered a problem doctrine has been a standard orthodox view for centuries. That is why it is helpful to ask: How old is the idea in the history of the Christian tradition? Where did it originate? What was it responding to? What were the original arguments disputing it? Understanding these contextual issues allows us to appreciate both the limits of an idea and how adaptive doctrines have been to the issues and context of the church throughout the centuries.

Jesus specialized in taking religious people's understandings about God and how everything works and then turning them on their heads. He wanted people to see that God was doing something new. In that vein, *Love Wins* stretches many of our preconceived ideas about Christianity for those both inside and outside the faith. Rob does this mostly by getting us to pay attention to what Jesus and his followers *actually* said. Embracing the biblical text with as much separation from our preexisting ideas and experiences as possible may offer some surprises about Jesus's good news. Perhaps God is offering a bigger love than many of us have ever imagined.

THE **LOVE WINS** COMPANION

CHAPTER ONE

WHAT ABOUT THE FLAT TIRE?

Overview by Rob Bell

Over the years I have met many people who are fascinated, compelled, or drawn to Jesus, but some reason or obstacle keeps them away. They may have heard from a Christian, "This is how it is, period, end of discussion. The Bible says it, so that settles it." Or they might have been taught that to follow Jesus, they had to go down a certain road and believe certain things, some of which they found problematic. What I'm interested in in this chapter is the power of questioning and the experience of solidarity in finding you're not alone—of always wondering, "But what about that?" and then finding out, "Oh, other people feel the same way."

My interest here is that you get loosened up with the questions, that the questions pull out of you, "You're right. That doesn't make sense" or "You're right. I've always had a problem with that explanation." It's okay. There should be no fear in the questioning and no hesitation in the asking. We can go there—that's the power.

And the biblical tradition is actually filled with questions, all the way to Jesus on the cross: "My God, my God, why have you forsaken me?" Questions are actually one of the ways we meet the divine. My hope is that somewhere in here you find your own questions and you learn that you aren't alone.

Going Deeper by David Vanderveen

Many readers of chapter 1 of *Love Wins* are a little taken back by all the questions Rob throws at them about what it means to be "saved." Rob is not trying to deny or criticize what Christians believe, but to reveal that our present understanding does not explain everything. Some churches suggest there is a specific process for getting "saved." In this chapter, Rob explores a wide range of those techniques, some of which conflict, as well as a long list of ways that Jesus told people they were accepted. Our beliefs about God, Jesus, and the meaning of Jesus's death and resurrection need to deepen in order for us to grasp more fully what the Bible means by "saved."

Rob is not the first to raise these issues. In a 1997 interview of evangelist Billy Graham by televangelist Robert Schuller of the "Hour of Power,"* the conversation was

* Find the interview online at http://www.youtube.com/watch?v=TNCnxA91fHE.

surprisingly broader than some Christians imagined it should be:

Schuller: Tell me, what do you think is the future of Christianity?

Graham: . . . I think everybody that loves Christ, or knows Christ, whether they're conscious of it or not, they're members of the Body of Christ. And I don't think that we're going to see a great sweeping revival that will turn the whole world to Christ at any time. I think James answered that, the Apostle James in the first council in Jerusalem, when he said that God's purpose for this age is to call out a people for His name. And that's what God is doing today. He's calling people out of the world for His name, whether they come from the Muslim world or the Buddhist world or the Christian world or the nonbelieving world, they are members of the Body of Christ, because they've been called by God. They may not even know the name of Jesus, but they know in their hearts that they need something that they don't have, and they turn to the only light that they have, and I think that they are saved, and that they're going to be with us in heaven.

Schuller: What I hear you saying is that it's possible for Jesus Christ to come into human hearts and souls and lives, even if they've been born in darkness and have never had exposure to the Bible. Is that a correct interpretation of what you're saying?

Graham: Yes, it is, because I believe that. I've met people in various parts of the world in tribal situations who have never seen a Bible or heard about a Bible and never heard of Jesus, but they've believed in their hearts that there was a God, and they've tried to live a life that was quite apart from the surrounding community in which they lived.

Schuller: I'm so thrilled to hear you say this. There's a wideness in God's mercy.

Graham: There is. There definitely is.

We should not be surprised that one of the greatest evangelists in the history of the church thought along these lines. As someone who had spent a career presenting the gospel to non-Christians, Graham had to think deeply and thoroughly about the logic of God's salvation. So should we.

We have included an excerpt from Oswald Chambers's *My Utmost for His Highest* as another example and model of a past Christian teacher who offers counsel. In "The Temptation of Religious Success," Chambers describes the danger of religious conformity and taking pride in Christian success. Instead, he advises that we try to seek only the Lord's approval. This is good, but tough advice.

People have very personal stories about how they came to accept Jesus or why they've rejected him. The questions, Bible studies, exercises, and readings in this chapter are designed to dig into the various claims different Christian groups make about what salvation is and the variety of ways to accomplish it, allowing you to explore more fully what you think the Bible teaches on this core issue. Before the group exercise and discussion questions, we have included a Bible study showcasing just how much the Bible embraces and models the practice of asking questions; this is followed by David Dark's reflections on the theme of his book, *The Sacredness of Questioning Everything,* which we excerpt.

Bible Study: A God Who Loves Questions

Many people are afraid to question their faith, having been taught that this is tantamount to either rejecting or losing one's faith. The best evidence against this line of thought is the Bible itself, in which both God and all the main characters ask many, many troubling questions. Asking questions is, in fact, a means God often uses to help us rid ourselves of limited and wrongheaded notions about God, so that we catch a larger and expanded vision of who we worship, which this survey of the Bible's use of questions reveals:

God [to Adam and Eve]: Where are you? . . . Who told you that you were naked? Have you eaten from the tree that I commanded you not to eat from? (Gen. 3:9–11)

Cain: Am I my brother's keeper? (Gen. 4:9)
God: What have you done? (Gen. 4:10)

Abraham: Will a son be born to a man a hundred years old? Will Sarah bear a child at the age of ninety? (Gen. 17:17)

God: Why did Sarah laugh and say, "Will I really have a child, now that I am old?" Is anything too hard for the LORD? (Gen. 18:13–14)

Moses: Suppose I go to the Israelites and say to them, "The God of your fathers has sent me to you," and they ask me, "What is his name?" Then what shall I tell them? (Exod. 3:13)

Job: Why does the Almighty not set times for judgment? Why must those who know him look in vain for such days? (Job 24:1)

God: Who is this that obscures my plans with words without knowledge? Prepare to defend yourself; I will question you, and you shall answer me. Where were you when I laid the earth's foundation? Tell me, if you understand. Who marked off its dimensions? Surely you know! Who stretched a measuring line across it? (Job 38:2–5)

Jeremiah: How long will the land lie parched and the grass in every field be withered? Because those who live in it are wicked, the animals and birds have perished. Moreover, the people are saying, "He will not see what happens to us."

God: If you have raced with people on foot and they have worn you out, how can you compete with horses? If you stumble in safe country, how will you manage in the thickets by the Jordan? (Jer. 12:4–5)

Habakkuk: How long, LORD, must I call for help, but you do not listen? Or cry out to you, "Violence!" but you do not save? Why do you make me look at injustice? Why do you tolerate wrongdoing? (Hab. 1:2–3)

Expert in the law: Teacher, what must I do to inherit eternal life?
Jesus: What is written in the Law? How do you read it? (Luke 10:25–26)

Jesus: Who do people say I am?
Disciples: Some say John the Baptist; others say Elijah; and still others, one of the prophets.
Jesus: But what about you? Who do you say I am? (Mark 8:27–29)

Jesus [to the Twelve]: You do not want to leave too, do you?
Peter: Lord, to whom shall we go? (John 6:67–68)

Jesus: You of little faith, why are you so afraid? [Then he got up and rebuked the winds and the waves, and it was completely calm.]
Disciples: What kind of man is this? (Matt. 8:26–27)

Jesus [on the cross]: *Eli, Eli, lema sabachthani?* (which means "My God, my God, why have you forsaken me?"). (Matt. 27:46)

Jesus: Simon son of John, do you love me more than these [fish]?

Peter: Yes, Lord, you know that I love you.

Jesus: Feed my lambs. . . . Simon son of John, do you love me?

Peter: Yes, Lord, you know that I love you.

Jesus: Take care of my sheep. . . . Simon son of John, do you love me?

Peter: Lord, you know all things; you know that I love you.

Jesus: Feed my sheep. (John 21:15–17)

Jesus: Saul, Saul, why do you persecute me?

Saul/Paul: Who are you, Lord? (Acts 9:4–5)

Paul: Are you so foolish? After beginning with the Spirit, are you now trying to finish by human effort? Have you experienced so much in vain? (Gal. 3:3–4)

James: Has not God chosen those who are poor in the eyes of the world to be rich in faith and to inherit the kingdom he promised those who love him? But you have dishonored the poor. Is it not the rich who are exploiting you? Are they not the ones who are dragging you into court? Are they not the ones who are blaspheming the noble name of him to whom you belong? (James 2:5–7)

John the letter writer: If any one of you has material possessions and sees a brother or sister in need but has no pity on them, how can the love of God be in you? (1 John 3:17)

Group Exercise: Knowing Your Story

Before engaging in the discussion questions below, take time to reflect on your own experiences and beliefs about conversion and salvation. How have you understood the role of conversion and salvation in your life? In the lives of others you know? What has been attractive about the idea of being "saved"? What has raised questions for you? What has seemed false? Spend time before the meeting writing down your own story about why you have embraced or rejected Jesus. Diagram or describe how you believe people get "saved" and what that means.

At the meeting, split up in groups of two or three and take the time to share each other's stories about being saved. After each person's story, the others in the group should provide feedback and reactions.

After everyone has shared their story, ask each other: How are our stories similar? How are they different? How did hearing others' stories shape or change how you think about what God's love and salvation might be about?

Discussion Questions

1. Before reading this book, how did you think of heaven and hell?
2. Do you believe God invites us, or even welcomes us, to discuss and debate the big questions of faith, doctrine, and the Bible?
3. Do you think Christians can know who does and who does not go to hell?

4. What messages have you heard about who goes (or how many go) to heaven? Or about how God can be both loving Father and Judge?
5. What percentage of people who have ever lived do you estimate will end up in hell? Do you think Gandhi is in hell?
6. What do you think non-Christians would say about the church's views on who goes and who does not go to heaven?
7. How do you respond to the problem Rob raises of explaining how a *finite* life of sin could entail *eternal* torment?
8. Do you believe there is no hope for atheists who die? Why or why not?
9. What role does our reason play in our salvation? What about people who are mentally handicapped, for example? How are they saved?
10. How important is the question, "Do you know where you will go after you die?" to your understanding of the Christian faith? Is "going somewhere else" (either heaven or hell) the message of Christianity?
11. Does our salvation depend on someone else sharing the good news of the gospel with us? Does others' salvation depend on our doing the same for them?
12. Of the questions Rob raises in this chapter, which did you experience as pertaining to issues you have had before or issues you would like to discuss more?

READING
QUESTIONING GOD
BY DAVID DARK

Do we really love God, or do we say we love God because we fear we will be damned otherwise? This nagging question, although primitive, nevertheless works its way into the souls of many Christians. Some respond by never letting questions arise; others deal with the questions by rejecting the faith. But what if God is actually the one behind the questions? What if God wants us to ask these questions? What if God actually loves questions? Such was the discovery of author and teacher David Dark, who writes about exactly these matters in his book The Sacredness of Questioning Everything *(Zondervan).*

Picture a tiny town with a tight-knit community. The people share joys and concerns, woes and gossip. They keep a close and often affectionate watch on one another's business. They talk and talk and talk.

What an outsider would notice within minutes of listening in on conversations are constant and slightly self-conscious references to "Uncle Ben." A beautiful sunset prompts a townsperson to say, "Isn't Uncle Ben awesome?" Good news brings out how thankful and overjoyed they feel toward Uncle Ben. Even in tragedy, a local might say, in a slightly nervous fashion, "You know, it just goes to show how much we all need Uncle Ben. I know—we all know—that Uncle Ben is good."

Uncle Ben is always on their minds.

Even when the magnificence of Uncle Ben isn't spoken of aloud, he's somehow present in facial expressions and actions. It's the look of stopping a train of thought before it goes too far, of letting an uncompleted sentence trail off into awkward silence, of swiftly hanging the subject. It's as if a conversation can only go so far. People hardly ever look one another in the eye for long.

At the beginning of each week there's a meeting in the largest house in town. Upon arriving, people get caught up in good fellowship and animated discussion of the week's events, with conversations straining in the direction of Uncle Ben. When a bell sounds, talk ceases. Everyone moves to the staircase and descends into the basement. Each person sits facing an enormous, rumbling furnace. Seated close to the furnace door, as if he were a part of the furnace itself, is a giant man in black overalls. His back is turned to them.

They wait in silence. In time the man turns around. His face is angry, contorted. He fixes a threatening stare of barely contained rage on each person, then roars, "Am I good?"

To which they respond in unison, "Yes, Uncle Ben, you are good."

"Am I worthy of praise?"

"You alone are worthy of our praise."

"Do you love me more than anything? More than anyone?"

"We love you and you alone, Uncle Ben."

"You better love me, or I'm going to put you . . . in here"—he opens the furnace door to reveal a gasping darkness—"forever."

Out of the darkness can be heard sounds of anguish and lament. Then he closes the furnace door and turns his back to them. They sit in silence.

Finally, feeling reasonably assured that Uncle Ben has finished saying what he has to say, they leave. They live their lies as best they can. They try to think and speak truthfully and do well by one another. They resume their talk of the wonders of Uncle Ben's love in anticipation of the next week's meeting.

But they're limited, in myriad ways, by fear. Fear causes them to censor their own thoughts and words. Fear prevents them from telling anyone of their inner anguish and fright. Fear keeps them from recognizing in one another's eyes their common desperation. This fear is interwoven, subtly and sometimes not so subtly, in all of their relationships.

End of story.

I find this story both jarring and entirely familiar. It captures some of my worst fears concerning the character of God. And I suspect a good number of people live their lives haunted by a nightmare similar to this one. Perhaps you entertain fears like these. Perhaps Uncle Ben forms your image of the divine even now.

Something akin to the Uncle Ben image might be what a lot of people refer to when they speak of religion as the worst thing that ever happened to them, a nightmare that damages everything it touches. We might protest that there's much more to religion than such tales of terror. But I find it hard to deny that the image of Uncle Ben lurks within an awful lot of what is called popular religious belief.

Uncle Ben might be the bestselling version of an all-powerful deity, a great and powerful Wizard of Oz type who refuses to be questioned and threatens anyone who dares to doubt or protest. Fear constrains many to call this God good and loving, ignoring what they feel inwardly. The less reverent candidly observe that this God is the perfect model for a brutal dictator, the cosmic crime boss who runs everything and expects us to be grateful. Trying to satisfy such a God while also getting through a workday, trying to balance a checkbook, and being moderately attentive to the needs of others can take a certain emotional toll.

Loving God

For a long time, I was in the habit of praying a prayer ("I love you, Lord") that was something of a gamble, like Pascal's wager. I wasn't sure I loved this God at all. In fact, I believed this Uncle Ben–like God was unlovable, determined to consign most of humanity to eternal torment for believing the wrong things. But, given the terrifying outcome of not loving him, it seemed sensible to say I loved and believed in him anyway. If, somehow, I succeeded in loving this God, lucky me. And if I didn't love him, I'd be more or less damned anyway.

Having faith in this brand of God is akin to Orwell's "double-think"—a disturbing mind trick by which we don't let ourselves know what's really going on in our minds for fear of what might follow. We learn to deny what we think and feel. The resulting mind-set is one of all fear all the time, a fear that can render us incapable of putting two and two together. Never quite free to *say* what we *see.*

When we think of belief intertwined with such fear, we might begin to wonder if self-professed believers caught in the grip of unseemly ideologies, religious or otherwise, are as fully convinced of what they claim to believe as they appear. Many are trying to prove their ultimate commitment by eliminating doubt—and fear—ridding themselves of the last vestiges of independent thought through force of will. Responding to the push that demands as much can become a kind of survival instinct. We do it without thinking about it. We witness the loss of independent thinking in a wide variety of settings—in offices, training camps, schools, political parties, clubs, families, and other religious assemblies. We're instructed to believe and to silence our questions and our imaginations. Like Orwell's Big Brother, Uncle Ben thrives when questioning is out of the question.

Open-ended questions such as "What on earth are we doing here?" and "Are we going crazy?" might occasionally give us enough air to keep breathing, but we're very often suffocating. We have just enough religion to be afraid as we go through our days, as we wake up and fall asleep. We feel pressure to believe—or pretend to believe—that God is love, while suspecting with a sinking feeling that God likes almost no one.

William Blake captured this hateful spirit most effectively by naming him Nobodaddy (nobody's daddy, nonfather, Father of Jealousy). As a being of hatefulness and perpetual accusation, Uncle Ben might be called a Satanic perversion of the idea of God. However we choose to name him, his voice (or its voice) is at work within our world.

For the record, I don't believe in the nonloving, fear-producing image that is Uncle Ben, but I hasten to add that I'm not without my own doubts. The intensity of the struggle ebbs and flows. When people ask, "Are you sure God isn't like Uncle Ben?" I tend to reply, "Most of the time."

Deliverance Begins with Questions

I readily confess that, in my darkest hours, the fear of an Uncle Ben, Nobodaddy-driven universe still has a hold on me, even as I hope and pray that my children and their children will find such an unworthy image of God to be almost comical. In my own religious upbringing, nobody ever told me that the Creator of the universe was a hellish handler of human beings. But as a child, I had a way of filling in the blanks with my imagination. Images sprang out of what I was told must be in the Bible somewhere. And some very dark ideas arose when talk of baptism and the age of accountability and assurance of salvation came up. I suppose such prospects motivated me, at least partially, to share my faith with other people. But would I really be doing others a favor if I managed to convince them of my own little nightmare? What should one do with a Nobodaddy on the brain? Is deliverance possible?

I believe deliverance begins with questions. It begins with people who love questions, people who live with questions and by questions, people who feel a deep joy when good questions are asked. When we meet these people—some living, some through history, art, and literature—things begin to change. Something is let loose. When we're exposed to the liveliness of holding everything up to the light of good questions—what I call "sacred questioning"—we discover that redemption is creeping into the way we think, believe, and see the world. This re-deeming (re-valuing) of what we've made of our lives, a redemption that perhaps begins with the insertion of a question mark beside whatever feels final and absolute and beyond questioning, gives our souls a bit of elbow room, a space in which to breathe and imagine again, as if for the first time.

I had specific convictions concerning God and sin and eternity, but I also understood that my concepts, however well I might articulate them, were flawed, broken and always in need of rehabilitation. When I heard Leonard Cohen proclaim in his song "Anthem" that there are cracks in absolutely everything, I sensed he was describing my life. The cracks, Cohen croons, as if we should all know it by now, are how the light shines in, and it is only by remaining aware of our imperfections that we remain open to redemption and reform. When we have questions, illumination is possible. Otherwise we're closed and no light can enter.

My inner Nobodaddy remained. Something clicked when a woman in Northern Ireland told me her own Uncle Ben story. She said she'd heard it from the Jesuit priest Gerard Hughes.* Until I heard her story, I didn't have a good way of talking about this binding, bad concept of God. I might even say that I didn't know this death-dealing negative image was there. I didn't know what had hold of me. The story, as stories will, prompted a lot of questions concerning the presumed goodness of God, the idea that God is love, and what it might mean to affirm, as I do, that God conquers rather than sponsors death.

The light began to shine through the cracks. Stories, I find, help the light to shine.

Sacred Questioning

There was a time in my life when I viewed the Uncle Ben story, despite its nightmarish quality, as an accurate depiction of the way things work. Protesting it would have seemed cosmically useless, given that this God doesn't suffer questions, doubts, or complaints. But I eventually came to suspect that any god who is nervous, defensive,

---

* Gerard Hughes speaks of "an identikit picture of God," which formed in his mind during his conversations with university students in his years as a chaplain. It became the story of "good old Uncle George." "Good old Uncle George" can be found in the first chapter of Hughes's book *Oh God, Why? A Spiritual Journey Towards Meaning, Wisdom, and Strength* (Abingdon, Oxfordshire, UK: Bible Reading Fellowship, 2000), http://www.gerardwhughes.com/oh_god_why_chapter1.htm (accessed August 21, 2008).

or angry in the face of questions is a false god. I began to realize that I often ascribed to God the traits of people who are ill at ease, anxious, and occasionally hateful and who even presume from time to time to speak on God's behalf. I began to wonder if the Bible backs up the contemptuousness they carry around.

Over time, the Bible ceased to be a catalog of all the things one has to believe (or pretend to believe) in order to not go to hell. Instead, the Bible became a broad, multifaceted collection of people crying out to God—a collection of close encounters with the God who is present, somehow, in those very cries. Far from being an anthology of greeting-card material, those accounts of joy, anger, lamentation, and hope are all bound upon the most formidable array of social criticism ever assembled in one volume.

And Christianity, far from being a tradition in which doubts and questions are suppressed in favor of uncritical, blind faith, began to assume the form of a robust culture in which anything can be asked and everything can be said. The call to worship is a call to complete candor and radical questioning—questioning the way things are, the way we are, and the way things ought to be. As G. K. Chesterton observed, the New Testament portrays a God who, by being wholly present in the dying cry of Jesus of Nazareth, even doubted and questioned himself. The summons to sacred questioning—like the call to honesty, like the call to prayer—is a call to be true and to let the chips fall where they may. This call to worship is deeper than the call to sign off on a checklist of particular tenets or beliefs. It is also more difficult.

READING
THE TEMPTATION OF RELIGIOUS SUCCESS
BY OSWALD CHAMBERS

It is good to be reminded we are not the first to be tempted by snags and dead ends in the Christian life. The church has had two millennia of practice. Here writer and preacher Oswald Chambers (1874–1917) provides a meditation on how we are tempted as Christians to measure ourselves by "successful service" or tempted to conform ourselves to "the pattern and print of the religious age we live in." Taken from his classic work My Utmost for His Highest, *his caution is timely as we think through what the real message of Jesus is and what constitutes ill-fitting tradition. His advice is also wise as well as relevant: focus solely to be approved by God, and work (and debate) with kindness and gentleness, without coercion. Amen.*

> Notwithstanding in this rejoice not, that the spirits are subject unto you. (Luke 10:20)

As Christian workers, worldliness is not our snare, sin is not our snare, but spiritual wantoning is, viz.: taking the pattern and print of the religious age we live in, making eyes at spiritual success. Never court anything other than the approval of God, go "without the camp, bearing His reproach." Jesus told the disciples not to rejoice in successful service, and yet this seems to be the one thing in which most of us do rejoice. We have the commercial view—so many souls saved and sanctified, thank God, now it is all right. Our work begins where God's grace has laid the foundation; we are not to save souls, but to disciple them. Salvation and sanctification are the work of God's sovereign grace; our work as His disciples is to disciple lives until they are wholly yielded to God. One life wholly devoted to God is of more value to God than one hundred lives simply awakened by His Spirit. As workers for God we must reproduce our own kind spiritually, and that will be God's witness to us as workers. God brings us to a standard of life by His grace, and we are responsible for reproducing that standard in others.

Unless the worker lives a life hidden with Christ in God, he is apt to become an irritating dictator instead of an indwelling disciple. Many of us are dictators, we dictate to people and to meetings. Jesus never dictates to us in that way. Whenever Our Lord talked about discipleship, He always prefaced it with an "IF," never with an emphatic assertion—"You must." Discipleship carries an option with it.

CHAPTER TWO

HERE IS THE NEW THERE

Overview by Rob Bell

What's fascinating to me is how many people, when you say the word *heaven,* immediately think, "Oh, that's the place that either does or doesn't exist, based on your story and your beliefs and your perspectives; it's the place that either does or doesn't exist when you die that is out there, over there, somewhere else." What I find terribly compelling is that when Jesus talked about heaven, he mostly talked about a dimension, a way of living, the accessibility of the life of God, right here, right now, in this world. For Jesus, heaven was far less about a speculation on what it will be like then and there and far more about a confidence that you, right now, can step into. Jesus called this "eternal life," which was a very rabbinical concept that meant living in conscious contact and communion with God right here, right now. Is that actually possible?

Was Jesus being truthful here? Can you actually step into a whole new kind of life right here, right now? Because if that's true, that raises all sorts of questions.

Going Deeper by David Vanderveen

Citing the Lord's Prayer, Rob connects "Your will be done on earth as it is in heaven" with the repeating promises in the Old and New Testaments that God is seeking partners to help move creation, so that it becomes a place where nothing competes with God's will to eradicate injustice from the earth, where all creation is restored.

Recently Bono, lead singer of the band U2, was interviewed by Bill Hybels, pastor of Willow Creek Church in Barrington, Illinois, about bringing heaven to earth:

Hybels: I read somewhere that when you say the Lord's Prayer, there's one phrase that really grips you; which one is it?

Bono: "Thy kingdom come *on earth* as it is in heaven."

Hybels: And why? Why does that one grab you?

Bono: Because a lot of people are happy with pie in the sky when they die, but I don't think that is what, um, is our purpose. Our purpose is to bring heaven to earth in the micro as well as the macro. In every detail of our lives, we should be trying to bring heaven to earth. Have the peace that passeth understanding at of the center of yourself, but do not be at peace with the world because the world is not a happy place for most people living on it. And the world is more malleable than you think, and we can wrestle it from fools.*

The idea that heaven is not a place out there that we will arrive at some day, but a reality we encounter now is at the heart of what Rob is writing about in *Love Wins.* How do we "bring heaven to earth," as Bono enjoins us? For many, being so steeped in an old model for heaven, this idea of heaven takes some getting used to. To help, we have included a Bible study on the heavenly visions from Isaiah, showing just how earthly these visions were.

Another teacher who helps us with this project is Bible scholar and bishop N. T. Wright. In an excerpt from a forthcoming book, *How God Became King,* Wright explains how seeing Jesus as teaching primarily about how we can get to heaven is one of the main reasons we cannot see the main story and themes of the Gospels.

Our ideas have consequences, and our beliefs about the last things shape how we live. If we want to participate actively in the ordering of creation with God (see Rev. 20), we must embrace a new idea of what heaven is and how close it is to our lives right here, right now.

Bible Study: Earthly Heavenly Visions

Once we remove our filters that only allow us to see heaven as a place we go to after leaving this world, we are then able to rediscover the rich narratives of the heavenly

* A transcript of the last part of that conversation, at 7:30 into the video: http://www.youtube.com/watch?v=grBByc7t3Fs.

yet earthly future visions of the prophets. A selection of passages from Isaiah are listed below. As you read these selections, notice the following: Where is God dwelling? Who is present there? What animals and things are listed as present? What are concrete signs that the day of the Lord has arrived? How do these images fit with how you think of heaven?

> In the last days
> the mountain of the LORD's temple will be
> established
> as the highest of the mountains;
> it will be exalted above the hills,
> and all nations will stream to it.
> Many peoples will come and say,
> "Come, let us go up to the mountain of the LORD,
> to the house of the God of Jacob.
> He will teach us his ways,
> so that we may walk in his paths."
> The law will go out from Zion,
> the word of the LORD from Jerusalem.
> He will judge between the nations
> and will settle disputes for many peoples.
> They will beat their swords into plowshares
> and their spears into pruning hooks.
> Nation will not take up sword against nation,
> nor will they train for war anymore. (2:2–4)

> The wolf will live with the lamb,
> the leopard will lie down with the goat,

the calf and the lion and the yearling together;
and a little child will lead them.
The cow will feed with the bear,
their young will lie down together,
and the lion will eat straw like the ox.
Infants will play near the hole of the cobra;
young children will put their hands into the viper's
   nest.
They will neither harm nor destroy
on all my holy mountain,
for the earth will be filled with the knowledge of
   the LORD
as the waters cover the sea. (11:6–9)

On this mountain the LORD Almighty will prepare
a feast of rich food for all peoples,
a banquet of aged wine—
the best of meats and the finest of wines.
On this mountain he will destroy
the shroud that enfolds all peoples,
the sheet that covers all nations;
he will swallow up death forever.
The Sovereign LORD will wipe away the tears
from all faces;
he will remove his people's disgrace
from all the earth.
The LORD has spoken. (25:6–8)

You will go out in joy
and be led forth in peace;
the mountains and hills

will burst into song before you,
and all the trees of the field
will clap their hands.
Instead of the thornbush will grow the juniper,
and instead of briers the myrtle will grow.
This will be for the LORD's renown,
for an everlasting sign,
that will endure forever. (55:12–13)

Discussion Questions

1. Rob remembers his grandmother's painting of heaven as a floating, glimmering city. What is your vision of heaven? What factors have shaped this vision?
2. How does the perception of our lives and our church change when we think of heaven as a restored earth rather than as a faraway place?
3. If Jesus consistently focused on heaven for today, why do we so emphasize heaven after we die?
4. Rob describes the Christian life as our preparation to become the kind of people who can dwell in heaven. How does this reorient how we shape our lives?
5. What is the connection between our understanding of heaven and how we live our lives?
6. In Matthew 19 when the rich man asks Jesus about "eternal life," what do you think the man had in

mind? What might Jesus mean by the term? What does "eternal life" mean to you?

7. If to "reign" with God means to "participate" with him in his creation, how might this inform our understanding of our calling in this life?
8. What does it mean that "eternal life" is available to us right here, right now?

READING
GOING TO HEAVEN?
BY N. T. WRIGHT

Rob argues that we misunderstand what Jesus meant by "eternal life"; it is not, he says, simply code for going to heaven after we die. In his forthcoming book, How God Became King: The Forgotten Story of the Gospels (HarperOne), *leading New Testament scholar N. T. Wright maintains that we have missed the central theme of the Gospels, because we have projected our own themes onto the text to explain what Jesus's main teaching was. One of the misinterpretations he writes about is the idea that Jesus was primarily concerned with who goes to heaven and how (and who does not).*

What have the churches normally done with "the middle bits" [of Jesus's life, the time between his birth and his death]? I have on occasion challenged groups of clergy and laity to tell me what they, or their congregations, might say if asked what "all that stuff in the middle" was about. What was the *point,* I have asked, of the healings and feastings, the Sermon on the Mount and the controversies with the Pharisees, the stilling of the storm and Peter's confession at Caesarea Philippi, and so on and so on—all the mass of rich material that the gospels offer us between Jesus's birth, or at least his baptism, and his trial and death? Pastors and preachers reading this book might like to ask themselves: If you asked your congregations about this, what do you think they would say? What, indeed, would your congregation expect *you* to say the gospels were all about?

The answers I have received have been revealing. The church's tradition has offered four forms of answer. None of them, I think, corresponds very closely to what the four gospels actually talk about. The first inadequate answer is that Jesus came to teach people how to go to heaven. This is, I believe, a major and serious misunderstanding.

Don't get me wrong. The whole New Testament assumes that God has a wonderful future prepared for his people after bodily death, climaxing in the new world of the resurrection, of new heavens and new earth. I have written about all that in detail elsewhere (especially in *Surprised by Hope*). But this is not—demonstrably not—what the four gospels are about.

The problem has arisen principally because for many centuries Christians in the Western churches at least have assumed that the whole point of Christian faith is to "go to heaven," so they have read everything in that light. To a man with a hammer, they say, all problems appear as nails. To a reader interested in post-mortem bliss, all scriptures seem to be telling you how to "go to heaven." But, as we shall see, they aren't.

This wrong reading has gained a good deal of apparent credibility from two expressions which occur regularly in the gospels, and which the western church at least has taken to refer to "heaven" in the traditional sense. The first expression is found frequently in Matthew's gospel. Because Matthew is the first gospel in the Canon, and has been from very early in the church's history, it exercises considerable influence on ordinary readers in how they understand the others as well. In Matthew, Jesus regularly speaks of "heaven's kingdom," whereas normally in the other gospels he speaks of "God's kingdom." Millions of readers, when they hear Matthew's Jesus talking about doing this or that "so that you may enter the kingdom of heaven" assume, without giving it a moment's thought, that this means "so that you may go to heaven when you die."

But that is not at all what Matthew, or Jesus for that matter, had in mind. Matthew makes it quite clear, and I think Jesus made it quite clear, what that phrase meant. Think of the Lord's Prayer, which comes at the center of the Sermon on the Mount in Matthew chapters 5–7. At the center of the prayer itself we find Jesus teaching his followers to pray that God's kingdom might come and his will be done "on earth as in heaven." The "kingdom of heaven" is not about people going to heaven. It is about the rule of heaven coming to earth. When Matthew has Jesus talking about heaven's kingdom, he means that heaven—in other words, *the God of heaven*—is establishing his sovereign rule not just in heaven, but on earth as well.

It is true that this phrase, "kingdom of heaven," seems to have been understood from quite early on in the church not in that first-century sense ("God's rule becoming a reality on this earth"), but in the quite different sense of "heaven" as a distant place where God ruled and to which he welcomed all those who followed Jesus. That seems to be already the case in the well-known hymn we call the "Te Deum Laudamus" ("We Praise Thee, O God"), which dates from at least as early as the fourth century. There we find the phrase (in the translation adopted by the Book of Common Prayer), "When thou hadst overcome the sharpness of death, thou didst open the kingdom of heaven to all believers." Read Matthew's gospel with *that* line in mind, and you are almost bound to see the "kingdom of heaven" as a place to which believers might have been barred because of sin, but to which now, through the death of Jesus, they have access. What's more, though the hymn does not exactly say so, it hints at a parallel: Jesus opened the "kingdom" through his death, so it is presumably through and after death that believers enter this "kingdom" themselves. That, one might risk a bet, is how generations of Christians have understood that bit of the "Te Deum" as they have said it or sung it. And it is a whole world away from what Matthew intended. It is as though you were to get a letter from the president of the United States inviting himself to stay at your home, and in your excitement you misread it and assumed that he was inviting you to stay at the White House.

The second expression that has routinely been misunderstood in this connection is the phrase "eternal life." For centuries within western culture, for the same reasons as before, people have simply assumed that the gospels are there to tell us "how to go to heaven." The word "eternity," in modern English and American, has regularly been used not only to point to that destination, but to say something specific about it, namely, that it will be somehow outside time, and probably outside space and matter as well. A disembodied, timeless eternity! That's what people have imagined. So when we find the Greek phrase *zoe aionios* in the gospels (and indeed in the epistles), and when it is regularly translated as "eternal life" or "everlasting life," people have assumed that that is the right way to understand it. "God so loved the world," reads the famous text in King James Version of John 3:16, "that he gave his only begotten Son, that whosoever believeth in him should not perish but have everlasting life."

But it isn't. In the many places where it comes in the gospels, and in Paul for that matter, the phrase *zoe aionios* refers to one aspect of an ancient Jewish belief in how time was divided up. In this viewpoint, there were two "aions" (we sometimes use the word "eons" in that sense): the "present age," *ha-olam hazeh* in Hebrew, and the "age to come," *ha-olam ha-ba*. The "age to come," many ancient Jews believed, would arrive one day, to bring God's justice, peace and healing to the world as it had groaned and toiled within the "present age." You can see Paul, for instance, referring to this idea in Galatians 1:4, where he speaks of Jesus giving himself for our sins "to deliver us from the present evil age." In other words, Jesus has inaugurated, ushered in, the "age to come." *But there is no sense that this "age to come" is "eternal" in the sense of being outside space, time and matter.* Far from it. The ancient Jews were creational monotheists. For them, God's great future purpose was not to rescue people out of the world, but to rescue the world itself, people included.

If we reframe our thinking within this setting, the phrase *zoe aionios* will refer to the "life of the age," in other words, the "life of the age to come." When the rich young ruler asks Jesus "Good teacher, what must I do to inherit eternal life?" he isn't asking how to go to heaven when he dies. He is asking about the new world that God is going to usher in, the new era of justice, peace and freedom God has promised his people. And he is asking, in particular, how he can be sure that when God does all this, he will be part of those who inherit the new world, who share its life. This is why, in my own new translation of the New Testament, John 3:16 ends, ". . . share in the life of God's new age."

Among the various results of this misreading has been the earnest attempt to make all the material in Jesus's public career refer somehow to a supposed invitation to "go to heaven" rather than to the present challenge of the kingdom coming on earth as in heaven. Time would fail to spell out the further misunderstandings that have resulted from this, but we might just note one. Jesus's controversies with his opponents, particularly the Pharisees, have regularly been interpreted on the assumption that the Pharisees had one system for "going to heaven" (in their case, keeping lots of stringent and fussy rules), and Jesus had another one, an easier path altogether in which God had relaxed the rules and made everything a lot easier. As many people are now aware, this does no justice either to the Pharisees or to Jesus. Somehow, we have to get our minds around a different, more challenging way of reading the gospels.

CHAPTER THREE

HELL

Overview by Rob Bell

We have tremendous power as human beings. We can choose all sorts of paths—we can choose peace, we can choose grace, we can choose love. We can also choose other paths, destructive paths, violent paths, abusive paths; we can choose to say no to the goodness of God's creation. Jesus had a way of talking about the power of this choice. He had a word he used to describe what happens when you reject the good, the true, the beautiful, the humane. The word Jesus used, and it was a word he used more than anybody else—in fact, he is one of the few people who use this word in the scriptures—is the word *hell*.

In this chapter I list how many times the word *hell* occurs, how Jesus uses the term, how other writers use it, and what it means for us today. My experience has been that the people who seem to talk the most about hell are talking about the hell after you die; they don't seem to talk much about the hell right now. But when Jesus talks about hell, he is mostly talking about a whole dimension to reality right now. So once again in the discussion, if we find ourselves caught up on "then," we are missing the dominant, compelling energy of Jesus's teachings, which is about the very real power of our choices right here, right now. And, again, the word he uses for this is *hell.*

Going Deeper by David Vanderveen

This chapter is about digging into what the Old and New Testaments actually say about hell. *Love Wins* covers every use of the actual word and related words as well as the contexts in which they are used in the Bible. (See the Bible Study below, which lists these verses.)

For Rob, hell is rooted in our ability to choose. There are a variety of literal hells-on-earth that people create here and now as well as a likely variety of hells that people can create later, after we die. God gives us the freedom to choose, even if that freedom means choosing hell, choosing separation from God.

Interestingly, *hell* is only used in the Bible when referring to God's chosen people—the elect, those who are "in." Jesus never uses *hell* to describe people outside Judaism. In the Old Testament stories of God's wrath and destruction, the wider context always points to a deeper plan of restoration. Even Sodom is restored in Ezekiel's visions.

Part of the discussion of hell in this chapter is also about what the word *eternal* and how the Greek words "*aion* of *kolazo*" are translated in many English Bibles as "eternal punishment." Many people read this Greek term to mean "punishment forever" or "ongoing punishment," which seems to miss the intentional healing, redemption, and love that God always includes when he talks about why he inflicts his wrath and punishment on his people.

Apart from English translations of the Greek for "eternal" and what that means, a bigger question might be: "What does *eternal* mean in English anymore?" Rob mentions new discoveries in modern physics, or string theory, in chapter 2, and the extra dimensions that must exist for our constantly expanding universe to exist. Brian Greene, a well-known string theorist at Columbia University, has said that space and time are really constructs for human organization of events and experience but are simply not fundamental laws of the universe. The idea of "eternal" meaning "forever," assuming a straightforward linear conception of time, isn't just a flawed concept in the English translations, it is as flawed a concept in the physical nature of the universe as the sun rotating around the earth. To let God be God and the universe be the universe, we must try to remove the influence of our limited perspectives from understanding the truth of the Bible and the cosmos.

Rob is clear that he affirms a real hell—a hell that reflects the scale of evil both from secrets hidden in our hearts and from the collapse and chaos of society when we fail to live in God's world, God's way. We are sometimes tempted to get so caught up in debates about what hell is like after we die that we overlook the earthly counterparts to damnation that haunt us today. That is what activist Shayne Moore deals with in the reading "Hell on Earth," which is taken from her book *Global Soccer Mom* (Zondervan).

Bible Study: (Almost) Everything the Bible Says About Hell

The three most pervasive references to the contemporary notion of hell* are derived from the Hebrew word *sheol,* the Greek word *hades,* and the Aramaic *gehenna.* The study below highlights how these words and their associated meanings are understood in the respective contexts. As you read, ask yourself: How does knowing the root meaning of these words change how you read them? What strikes you as you read all these verses together?

Sheol

Sheol is used throughout the Old Testament in reference to the underworld, the grave, or the abode of the dead, where there is no praise of God. The term resembles the parallel Greek term *hades* in that it is the common receptacle of the dead. (English translations of *sheol* are italicized.)

* The Old Testament references are abundant and its meaning redundant. Therefore, for the sake of brevity, those included reflect a selected portion that remain consistent with the overall usage of the term.

All his sons and daughters came to comfort him, but he refused to be comforted. "No," he said, "in mourning will I go down to *the grave* to my son." So his father wept for him. (Gen. 37:35)

But Jacob said, "My son will not go down there with you; his brother is dead and he is the only one left. If harm comes to him on the journey you are taking, you will bring my gray head down to *the grave* in sorrow." (Gen. 42:38)

For a fire will be kindled by my wrath,
one that burns down to the *realm of the dead*
below.
It will devour the earth and its harvests
and set afire the foundations of the mountains.
(Deut. 32:22)

The Lord brings death and makes alive;
he brings down to *the grave* and raises up.
(1 Sam. 2:6)

If only you would hide me in *the grave*
and conceal me till your anger has passed!
If only you would set me a time
and then remember me! (Job 14:13)

If the only home I hope for is *the grave,*
if I spread out my bed in the realm of
darkness . . . (Job 17:13)

They spend their years in prosperity
and go down to *the grave* in peace. (Job 21:13)

Among the dead no one proclaims your name.
Who praises you from *the grave*? (Ps. 6:5)

Because you will not abandon me to the *realm of the dead,*
nor will you let your faithful one see decay. (Ps. 16:10)

Let me not be put to shame, LORD,
for I have cried out to you;
but let the wicked be put to shame
and be silent in *the realm of the dead.* (Ps. 31:17)

You boast, "We have entered into a covenant with death,
with the *realm of the dead* we have made an agreement." . . .
"Your covenant with death will be annulled;
your agreement with the *realm of the dead* will not stand.
When the overwhelming scourge sweeps by,
you will be beaten down by it." (Isa. 28:15, 18)

For the grave cannot praise you,
death cannot sing your praise;
those who go down to *the pit*
cannot hope for your faithfulness. (Isa. 38:18)

Indeed, wine betrays him;
he is arrogant and never at rest.
Because he is as greedy as *the grave*

> and like death is never satisfied,
> he gathers to himself all the nations
> and takes captive all the peoples. (Hab. 2:5)

Hades

Literally, *haides* means "not to be seen." The Greek *haidou* (possessive) means "the house of Hades." On its own (as a subject) it designates the abode of the dead. In the New Testament Hades assumes a provisional character and is never employed in connection with the final state of punishment subsequent to the last judgment.

> And you, Capernaum, will you be lifted up to the skies? No, you will go down to the *depths*. If the miracles that were performed in you had been performed in Sodom, it would have remained to this day. (Matt. 11:23; cf. Luke 10:15)

> And I tell you that you are Peter, and on this rock I will build my church, and the gates of *death* will not overcome it. (Matt. 16:18)

> In *Hades,* where he was in torment, he looked up and saw Abraham far away, with Lazarus by his side. (Luke 16:23)

> Because you will not abandon me to the *realm of the dead,*
> you will not let your holy one see decay. (Acts 2:27)

> Seeing what was to come, he spoke of the resurrection of the Messiah, that he was not abandoned to the *realm of the dead,* nor did his body see decay. (Acts 2:31)

> I am the Living One; I was dead, and now look, I am alive for ever and ever! And I hold the keys of death and *Hades*. (Rev. 1:18)

> I looked, and there before me was a pale horse! Its rider was named Death, and *Hades* was following close behind him. They were given power over a fourth of the earth to kill by sword, famine and plague, and by the wild beasts of the earth. (Rev. 6:8)

> The sea gave up the dead that were in it, and death and *Hades* gave up the dead that were in them, and everyone was judged according to what they had done. (Rev. 20:13)

Gehenna

Gehenna is derived from the literal Valley of Hinnom, located by different writers in one of three great valleys around Jerusalem. In all cases, it designates the place of punishment of the wicked. It is associated with fire and, in some cases, destruction.

> But I tell you that anyone who is angry with a brother or sister will be subject to judgment.

Again, anyone who says to a brother or sister, "Raca," is answerable to the Sanhedrin. And anyone who says, "You fool!" will be in danger of the fire of *hell*. (Matt. 5:22)

If your right eye causes you to stumble, gouge it out and throw it away. It is better for you to lose one part of your body than for your whole body to be thrown into *hell*. And if your right hand causes you to stumble, cut it off and throw it away. It is better for you to lose one part of your body than for your whole body to go into *hell*. (Matt. 5:29–30)

Do not be afraid of those who kill the body but cannot kill the soul. Rather, be afraid of the One who can destroy both soul and body in *hell*. (Matt. 10:28)

And if your eye causes you to stumble, gouge it out and throw it away. It is better for you to enter life with one eye than to have two eyes and be thrown into the fire of *hell*. (Matt. 18:9; cf. Mark 9:47)

Woe to you, teachers of the law and Pharisees, you hypocrites! You travel over land and sea to win a single convert, and then you make that convert twice as much a child of *hell* as you are. (Matt. 23:15)

> You snakes! You brood of vipers! How will you escape being condemned to *hell*? (Matt. 23:33)

> If your hand causes you to stumble, cut it off. It is better for you to enter life maimed than with two hands to go into *hell,* where the fire never goes out. (Mark 9:43)

> But I will show you whom you should fear: Fear him who, after your body has been killed, has authority to throw you into *hell.* Yes, I tell you, fear him. (Luke 12:5)

> The tongue also is a fire, a world of evil among the parts of the body. It corrupts the whole person, sets the whole course of one's life on fire, and is itself set on fire by *hell.* (James 3:6)

Group Exercise: The Hell Download

Hell can be an emotional and heavy topic to discuss. It will help to air some of these feelings and associations before beginning the discussion questions. Split up into groups of twos and threes and take turns answering these questions:

- What were you taught about hell? How have you understood it in the past?
- What most scares you about the topic?
- Were you ever worried that someone you knew or loved was in hell? Describe that experience.

The goal is for people to get out into the open all the heaviness and baggage we bring to this laden topic. This can both inform our responses to the questions below and sensitize us to others' context on the subject.

Discussion Questions

1. What were your concepts of hell prior to reading *Love Wins*? What factors have shaped this vision? Has your concept of hell changed over time and, if so, how?
2. Rob describes how Old Testament and Hebrew uses of words related to "hell," words like "Sheol" and "Hades," were very different from what the New Testament means by "hell." How are they different, and what do you think is significant about these differences?
3. Why do you think Judaism was less focused on defining hell as judgment and torment the way some modern Christians do? How might these differences in understanding our final state change how we approach our faith in God and how we understand our religious lives?
4. Rob teaches that hell is real, both in this life and in the life after death. What do you think it means for there to be hell on earth today? Have you ever witnessed something you would describe as "hell"? What does calling something hell in this life change how you see that reality?

5. What do you think is accomplished if God's judgment lasts forever without restoration? What would be the purpose? What do you think of the idea that hell might be for correction rather than as punishment? If the purpose of hell is for correction, then what do you think happens in hell?
6. What changes in how you think of the gospel when hell is seen as temporary or for a limited time?
7. Rob offers some different meanings for the phrase "*aion* of *kolazo*," which he claims gets mistakenly translated to mean "eternal punishment." What do you think the Bible means by "eternal"? What changes if we think of "eternal" as measuring something other than chronological time?
8. If we remove the threat of punishment in our presentation of the gospel, why might someone be interested in the good news?
9. How have your beliefs about hell changed through studying this chapter? How have they stayed the same? Does it change how you view the character of God, including your relationship to him and to others in this life?

READING
BECOMING A DEEP READER OF SCRIPTURE
BY CLAYTON LIBOLT

Love Wins *is primarily about the big picture of God's story for us as told in the Bible, particularly in the Gospels. Some critics have debated Rob Bell's interpretations of scripture, particularly his discussion of* heaven, hell, *and the* permanence of death *as they relate to salvation. Dr. Clayton Libolt is the head pastor at River Terrace Church in East Lansing, Michigan. He has a Ph.D. in Ancient Near Eastern Languages and Literature from the University of Michigan. This original essay for the companion deals with the very real problem of how we avoid "misreading" the Bible when we do not have degrees in biblical studies and are not fully aware of the historical and literary context of the passages we are trying to understand. Is the Bible too complicated to read on our own unless we are biblical experts? As you will see, his answer is no, but there are things we can do to become better readers of the Bible.*

Most people approach the Bible with an idea about what it says already in mind. They may have picked up these preconceptions from the movies or from Sunday school or sermons. Or maybe it's just what they expect God would say.

A lot of people think the Bible is about dos and don'ts. *Do this. Don't do that*—as if God were mostly concerned about managing our lives.

Others expect the main topic to be heaven and hell—how to get in the one and avoid the other. For still others, it's all about developing a personal relationship with Jesus. Or it's a book of doctrine.

Whatever the idea, people come to the Bible expecting to find *that,* and when they don't, it can be terribly confusing. They say, "I've tried reading the Bible, but I don't get anything out of it."

At that point some people put their Bible on a shelf and stop reading. Others find ways to make their Bibles say what they expect and want to hear. If it's dos and don'ts you want, concentrate on passages like Exodus 20 (the Ten Commandments), the book of Deuteronomy, and Matthew 5. If it's hell, read the end of the last parable in Matthew 25, the part of John 15 that talks about the branches being hacked off and burned, and Revelation 20:11–15 with its lake of fire, and you get a fire-and-brimstone Bible. If you are looking for doctrine, read a lot of Paul and avoid the first three Gospels.

This will work for a while, but if you read the Bible long enough and deeply enough, with an open heart and open mind, the Bible will eventually get you to rethink what you thought it wants to teach you when you started to read. The Bible has a way of challenging our ideas—even the ideas we learned in church—and opening up for us new ways to see and understand God, the world, and our own lives.

Love Wins, Rob Bell's fine book, is about this kind of reading. It's about rediscovering the story of the Bible and finding that the story is much better than he, Rob Bell, or we thought. Better than the story he had been taught. Probably better than the story you have been taught.

But can we believe it? How do we evaluate, explore, and extend Rob's reading of the Bible? Any good telling of the biblical story should drive us back to the Bible itself. And that's the purpose of this essay: to invite you into your own reading of the Bible and along the way to give you a few tools and hints you may find useful for your reading.

How Do You Get to the Maccabean Martyrs?

In chapter 2 of *Love Wins,* Rob explores the story of the rich young ruler, the young man who asked Jesus, "What good thing must I do to get eternal life?" (That's Matthew's phrasing of the question in 19:16; Mark and Luke phrase it differently.) The story gives Rob the opportunity to examine the biblical concept of eternal life. Just what is the young man asking for? What is "eternal life"?

How would you approach the eternal life question? You could do a biblical word study (and we will a little later in this essay), but before you do a word study, check out a commentary, or look at the notes at the bottom of your study Bible, you should do something else: *get acquainted with the deep background of the New Testament.*

For people living in the first and second centuries, looking into the deep background of the times of Jesus wasn't necessary. They were still living it. But for us, for people of the twenty-first century, especially people steeped in what they have been taught in Sunday school since they were small, it's important. We need to rediscover the Jewishness of Jesus.

This is a great time to do that. Over the past few decades, much has been learned about the cultural background of the New Testament. A rich trove of primary and secondary materials has accumulated. Many scholars have worked through these materials, and much of what they have discovered is accessible to nonscholars.

By background, you may think first about the Old Testament. The Old Testament is important, but not the Old Testament by itself. Of greater importance is how the Old Testament was read and understood in Jesus's day. For that we have a wealth of sources, some of them known since the beginning of the Christian era and some, like the Dead Sea Scrolls, known only within the last century.

Out of these materials a picture has emerged. The picture is of a Jesus very much engaged with the questions of his day, questions that include the future of the covenant people, why they continued to suffer, how the kingdom that God had promised would come at last, and when the new age would begin.

Go back to the story of the rich young ruler. The question the young man asks doesn't come out of the blue. It's part of a larger conversation that goes back to the time of the Maccabean revolt (167–164 BCE).

People of Jesus's day were steeped in the martyr stories that came out of the period of the Maccabees. Two stories stand out. The first is about a ninety-year-old religious teacher and leader named Eleazar. The second, about a mother and her seven sons (2 Macc. 6–7 in Roman Catholic and Orthodox Bibles, and a more elaborate version in 4 Maccabees, included in many editions that include a separate section for the Apocrypha).

The second story is particularly stunning. Refusing to compromise their faith by eating pork, each of the sons is, in turn, from oldest to youngest, brutally tortured and killed. As they go to their deaths, they express their confidence that God will vindicate them and give them new life.

Brave as the sons are, it's the mother who stands out. In 4 Maccabees she gets the final, summing-up speech. The author says of her: "As though she had a mind of adamant and were this time bringing her brood of sons to birth into immortal life, she encouraged them and pled with them to die for piety's sake."* The same author adds, ". . . They now stand beside the divine throne and live the life of the age of blessing."†

"They now stand beside the divine throne and live the life of the age of blessing." When the rich young ruler approaches Jesus and asks, "What good thing must I do to have eternal life?" it's these Maccabean martyr stories that are swirling around the story. "Tell me, Jesus, what do I have to do?" the young man asks. "Do I have to die? Be tortured? What good thing must I do to stand beside the divine throne and live the life of the age of blessing?"

---

* James H. Charlesworth, ed., *The Old Testament Pseudepigrapha,* vol. 2, trans. H. Anderson (Garden City, NY: Doubleday, 1985), p. 561.

† Charlesworth, ed., *Old Testament Pseudepigrapha,* vol. 2, p. 563.

And now you can see why the answers of Jesus are so disappointing to the young man. It's not that they are so hard—keep the commandments, give your goods to the poor, follow Jesus—it's that they are in a way too easy. They don't require any, well, heroism. They ask the rich young man to step back, assume the role of a servant, become just one of *those*—an unwashed disciple of Jesus.

We can leave the story here, at least for the moment. There is more to be said, but the story itself is not the question in front of us. The question is how, if you pick up a Bible and start to read, do you get to the Maccabean martyrs and connect their story to the story of the rich young ruler? Or how, in any part of the gospel story, do you catch enough of the cultural conversation so you understand what the question is?

Take another example. In the same chapter of Matthew—Matthew 19—Jesus is standing just across the Jordan from Judea. He is ready to enter Judea for the last time and to die. But before he dies, he goes back to where the whole adventure started, where he was baptized by his cousin John, where he heard the voice of the Father, and where the Spirit descended on him.

Just there one of the religious leaders decides to ask him a question about divorce: "Is it lawful for a man to divorce his wife for any and every reason?" Why there? Why that question?

Because it was there that John stood when he condemned the divorce of Herod Antipas and his marriage to his brother's wife. And it's there, according to Matthew 14:3–5, that Herod had John arrested and waited for a pretext to kill him. The question isn't about just any divorce; it's about *that* divorce. "Jesus," the man was asking, "do you have the courage to do what John did? Do you have the courage to condemn the divorce and marriage of Herod?"

Jesus answers in no uncertain terms. He calls what Herod did adultery. But to take this passage out of the context of this discussion—the religious, political, social context—and apply it to just any marriage that comes apart, as if Jesus were here legislating for all time, loses what is going on in this passage.

If we are to read the Gospels well, it's important for us to catch as much of the cultural conversation as we can. So how do we do that? How do we catch the conversation about the Maccabean martyrs buzzing around the story of the rich young ruler and the gossip about Herod marrying his brother's wife swirling around the question about divorce? How do we get to that information, so that our reading of the Gospels is better informed, closer, we hope, to what they were written to say?

Let me suggest three things you might do. First, get yourself a good orientation to the culture out of which the Gospels arose. You need an introduction, a way to get your bearings. I would suggest reading N. T. Wright, the Anglican Bible scholar who has written widely about Jesus and Jesus's world in books intended for nonspecialists as well as specialists.

The big book, part of an even bigger series of books, is *Jesus and the Victory of God*.* This book will give you

---

* N. T. Wright, *Jesus and the Victory of God* (Minneapolis: Fortress, 1996).

not only Wright's own orientation to Jesus and the world of first-century Palestine, but also a review of what other scholars have said and thought. A smaller, more accessible book is Wright's *Simply Jesus: A New Vision for Who He Was, What He Did, and Why He Matters.** Either of these books is a way to access a conversation—a conversation that has been going on for years now—about Jesus and how Jesus did and did not fit into his own time.

Jesus was in conversation with the cultural currents of his time. He was not a spaceman dropped out of another dimension into this one with no knowledge of what was going on. He was a first-century Jew. This is what incarnation means. To understand his age helps us to better understand him.

So, first, get a good orientation to the time in which Jesus lived. Second, read broadly. Not just the New Testament, but the Old Testament, especially the prophets (parts of Zechariah read like a script for Holy Week). And not just the Old Testament, but the Apocrypha (found in Roman Catholic and Orthodox Bibles). And not just the Apocrypha, but the Pseudepigrapha (available in many academic or ecumenical Bibles that have a section with the entire Apocrypha). And if you have time and taste for more, read a bit into the Dead Sea Scrolls. These and other writings provide the deep literary context for the New Testament.

And last—this is most important—read the Bible. Not small selected passages. Not just what is familiar. Not the

---

* N. T. Wright, *Simply Jesus: A New Vision for Who He Was, What He Did, and Why He Matters* (San Francisco: HarperOne, 2011).

kind of passages that prove your point. Read the Bible in great swaths, books at a time. Listen as if for the first time. What are you hearing here? What are the themes? The literary devices? The *poetry* of the text?

Recently in Scotland I had the opportunity to listen in while a small group reported on their reading of the first half of Isaiah—thirty-three chapters. For one man, new to the faith, it was his first time. It was fascinating to listen to his observations on the sweep and grandeur of the text.

The goal of our reading of the Bible should be what T. S. Eliot said of life itself:

> We shall not cease from exploration
> And the end of all our exploring
> Will be to arrive where we started
> And know the place for the first time.
>
> "Little Gidding," from *Four Quartets*

Checking Out the Words (and the Words on the Words)

Frequently in *Love Wins,* Rob Bell leads us on a hunt for the precise meaning of a word or phrase—"heaven," "hell," "eternal life," and others—words that we assume we know the meanings of, but that in fact turn out to have meanings quite different from what we assumed. This is the second step in our Bible adventure: getting at the words.

Some basics. The Bible was written over a long period time in three languages: Hebrew (most of the Old Testament), Aramaic (parts of the books of Daniel and Ezra), and Greek (the New Testament). One complication: the

New Testament writers knew and often used a Greek translation of the Old Testament known to us as the Septuagint, so in accounting for what a given word means in the New Testament, we have to keep in mind not only what the word meant in the Greek of that day, but how it was used in the Septuagint, which for many first-century Jews was the Bible, and what Hebrew (or occasionally Aramaic) word underlies the Greek.

The following is the simple approach to searching key words (a more detailed description and rationale are given below):

1. Pick the word you wish to research. For this example, we will use the word "hell."
2. Go to http://www.blueletterbible.org, pick a translation (we'll use the King James Version, or KJV, for this exercise), and enter the word "hell."
3. "Hell" is used to translate several Hebrew and Greek words in the KJV. You'll notice numbers, known as Strong's numbers, next to each use of the word "hell." You can click on each reference and see the variety of original words translated as "hell" in the KJV as well as their uses. For example, you'll notice that "Sheol" is used in Deuteronomy 32:22, but the word "Sheol" does not mean a place of fire or torment.
4. Take the time to reference a variety of words and their meanings across a variety of biblical translations that come up in *Love Wins* or in your own study

of the Bible. There is great depth of meaning in the original texts that may surprise you.

This may seem terribly complicated, and it can be, but it may be plainer if we use an example. Take the Greek word *hades*. It is used just ten times in the New Testament: Matthew 11:23; 16:18; Luke 10:15; 16:23; Acts 2:27, 31; Revelation 1:18; 6:8; 20:13, 14 (some manuscripts also have it in 1 Cor. 15:55).

In the KJV, it's always translated "hell." Modern versions take a variety of strategies. The New International Version (NIV, 2011 edition), for example, sometimes translates it "realm of the dead," but more often uses the word itself, "Hades." But what does it mean, this word we still use rather carelessly in our casual speech? Let's go through the steps.

Begin with identifying the texts. I've listed them above, but what if they weren't listed? How would you know how many times and where the word *hades* was used in the New Testament?

Start with the English. Say you are using the KJV, and you are researching the word "hell." You need to find out how often and where the word "hell" is used in your Bible.

For that you need a concordance. A concordance is a list of the words of a book, in this case the Bible, usually in alphabetical order, citing where that word occurs in the text. Bibles often have small concordances at the back, but these won't do. They are not comprehensive. You need a concordance that cites all instances of the word.

In general circulation there are two old books that do just this, *Young's Analytical Concordance to the Bible* and *Strong's Exhaustive Concordance to the Bible*. These are keyed to the KJV. There are also lots of Bible software packages and online resources that can search the Bible, many of them keyed to modern translations as well as the KJV.

For our purposes, we are going to use the website http://www.blueletterbible.org. When the website comes up, we pick a version (in this case, the KJV) and we enter our word, "hell." We hit the search button, and the results come up on the screen: all the instances of the word "hell" in the KJV, both Old Testament and New Testament.

Since we are interested in "hell" in the New Testament, we scroll down to the New Testament results, and we discover that "hell" is used not ten times, as I said above, but twenty-three times. What's going on?

The answer is that "hell" in the KJV is used to translate several different Greek words. On the Blue Letter Bible website, each word is associated with a number. These are known as the "Strong's" numbers, because they come from *Strong's Exhaustive Concordance,* mentioned above. If you look carefully you will see that the "hell" citations have three different numbers associated with them: 1067, 86, and 5020. (Or you can click on a tab marked "Lexi-Conc," which will show what Greek or Hebrew word each number represents.)

Click on the first of these numbers, found, for example, in the citation of Matthew 5:22, and what comes up is *geenna* (Gehenna). Interesting, but we are hunting down *hades,* not Gehenna. Click on the next number, 86, found alongside the word "hell" in the citation of Matthew 11:23, and up comes *hades* (Hades).

On this page, the Blue Letter Bible presents some important information. It gives an "outline of biblical usage," in this case three short definitions of the word *hades.* Below, it gives its source for these definitions, Thayer's *Lexicon.* Below that, it lists the passages where *hades* occurs.

We would seem to be there—at our definition of *hades.* But we are not. First of all, Thayer's *Lexicon* is really old. Some would say obsolete, written before much was known about the kind of Greek that is used in the New Testament. Second, we haven't taken account of how the word *hades* was used in, you guessed it, the Septuagint. Or in the Hebrew. For that we have to go back to our website Bible concordance, the Blue Letter Bible.

Go back to the search results, but this time to the Old Testament results. Take the first citation, Deuteronomy 32:22, "For a fire is kindled in mine anger, and shall burn unto the lowest hell" (KJV). Click on the Strong's number, 7585.

What comes up is a page for *she'owl* (Sheol). We find the same sort of information we found with the *hades* page: an "outline of biblical usage," a citation from a lexicon, this time Gesenius (another really old lexicon), and a list of the citations for "Sheol." The Gesenius citation tells us one thing more: that *sheol* in Hebrew roughly corresponds to *hades* in Greek, and that both of them mean the place where the dead go.

The best thing to do at this point is to read through the passages. Read through them not simply in the KJV, but in a variety of modern versions. Study the way the word is used.

What you will discover, should you do this, is that "Sheol" in the Old Testament is not anything like what English-speaking people think of when they use the word "hell." It's not a lake of fire with devils standing around with pitchforks. It doesn't look like the thousands of cartoons that have depicted hell in the *New Yorker*. It's more cold than hot, more shadowy than defined, more universal than particular. And it's this concept, not the picture of hell swimming around in our imaginations, that underlies the New Testament concept of *hades*.

Underlies it, but doesn't entirely explain it. There was a great deal of development of the concept of *hades* in the period between, say, the first and second destructions of Jerusalem (586 BCE, 70 CE). If we are to get a full grasp of the New Testament use of the word *hades,* we also need this information.

But by now something should have occurred to us: that maybe "hell" is not a good translation of *hades*. And when someone reads the KJV, which has "hell" for *hades,* what is likely to happen is something gets read into the Bible that really isn't there. If we are to grasp what is there, we have to step back and reexamine what is being said.

So far, the result of our little experiment in word study is mostly negative: what the word, in this case, *hades*, does not mean. If we want to proceed with our study, we have to do two more things: first, check out what the latest scholarship says about the word and, second, get a grasp on how the concept of *hades* played in the first century when the New Testament was being written. For these things, we need something more.*

Consulting the Community

We don't or shouldn't do Bible study alone. So far we have put in place two things: the deep cultural background to the New Testament and our own personal knowledge of the texts (our word study). It's time to access the work of others—to go to commentaries, study Bibles, and whatever else we can find.

But be careful. Don't begin with one of those older, dogmatic commentaries that are so popular. Not because they don't contain much of value. They often do, but we are not ready for them yet. What we want at this point are commentaries and notes that open up the text, that inform rather than defend a point of view, that call our attention to the background of the text rather than make application to life.

And always be ready to question whether what the commentator is saying is true or not. After all, by now you have a firm grounding in background materials. You have done your own research on some of the key words.

Ask yourself, does this commentary, study Bible, or other aid to reading provide credible information beyond

---

* You can get a clue by reading the entry for *hades* in Gerhard Kittel and Gerhard Friedrich, eds., *Theological Dictionary of the New Testament,* abridged in one volume, trans. Geoffrey W. Bromiley (Grand Rapids, MI: Eerdmans, 1985).

what you already know? Does it provide insights into the text that you otherwise would have missed?

You should also do this with Rob Bell's book. *Love Wins* is a reading of the New Testament—not just about heaven and hell—but about the center of the faith. Check out what Rob says. Read the texts he cites. Read around the texts he cites. Is he getting at the heart of it?

And—this is important—look for what he has missed. One of the claims Rob makes is that death does not finally decide eternity—that even beyond death there are possibilities. Rob cites Matthew 19, Acts 3, and Colossians 1 as texts that point in that direction along with other texts.

But he may have missed an important one. While I was writing this essay, one of my colleagues brought to me 1 Corinthians 15:29: "Now if there is no resurrection, what will those do who are baptized for the dead? If the dead are not raised at all, why are people baptized for them?" (NIV). This is admittedly a difficult text, but on a straightforward reading, it seems to countenance change after death. If we add to this verse what precedes it ("For he [Christ] must reign until he has put all his enemies under his feet. The last enemy to be destroyed is death," 1 Cor. 15:25–26, NIV), we have a strong argument that death is not the limit we usually take it to be.

The point is not the interpretation of 1 Corinthians 15:29 that I just proposed; the point is that in reading a book like *Love Wins* we have to be alert not only to what it says, but to what it may have missed. Think of reading *Love Wins* as a conversation, a conversation with a passionate preacher who loves the gospel. Read, appreciate, question, challenge, and learn.

So now we have three things to help us in our in our interpretation of the Bible: the deep background, our own careful and intensive study, and the suggestions and help provided by the interpretative community. This may be enough, but if our interpretation is to soar, we need one more thing: a Spirit-filled creativity.

Dancing with the Rock

One of the most creative moves made by Rob Bell is his interpretation of 1 Corinthians 10 (143ff.). In this passage, Paul introduces the Old Testament story of the rock in the wilderness and then says, stunningly, "the rock was Christ" (10:4). Rob mentions that nothing in the Old Testament story itself would seem to point to Jesus as the rock, but, Rob adds, "Paul, however, reads another story in the story, insisting that Christ was present in that moment, that Christ was providing the water they needed to survive—that Jesus was giving, quenching, sustaining" (143).

He goes on to ask whether Christ is present in hidden ways in other places and other times—whether, in other words, we have a far too limited idea of who Christ is and where he appears.

Some of Rob's critics have taken him to task for this interpretation of the passage. They claim that his interpretation lacks seriousness. It's not sober-minded enough. But in fact the church has for its whole history seen Christ in the Old Testament in just this way. The church has believed that God's work is seamless: it is all Christ's work, whether Old or New Testament, whether yesterday or today or tomorrow.

The Bible invites a playful creative reading. It asks us to dance with the rock, to see that our staid interpretations often risk missing the creativity of God himself. Which is to say, in conclusion, that our readings should always be filled with delight, discovery, prayerful appreciation of a God who does not give up on Abraham or Sarah, David or Bathsheba, Peter or Mary Magdalene. Or on you or me.

And that is good news, good news indeed.

READING
HELL ON EARTH
BY SHAYNE MOORE

What some readers miss in Love Wins *is that Rob is not arguing that there is no hell. Instead, he teaches that Jesus insists that hell is very real—uncomfortably real, in fact. But he insists that Jesus did not mean hell is merely a place souls go after people die. Instead, hell is a consequence of people choosing not to follow the path of life God puts before us; by rejecting God, we are free to create hell—both on earth and after death. And to worry about who goes to hell after death while ignoring the hells on earth is massively to miss God's point—as activist Shayne Moore reveals in this excerpt from her book* Global Soccer Mom: Changing the World Is Easier Than You Think *(Zondervan).*

Africa, 2005

> It was a strongly held belief of most first-century Jews, and virtually all early Christians, that history was going somewhere under the guidance of God and that where it was going was toward God's new world of justice, healing, and hope. The transition from the present world to the new one would be a matter not of the destruction of the present space-time universe but of its radical healing.
>
> N. T. Wright, *Surprised by Hope*

- Undernutrition contributes to almost half of all child deaths and more than 20 percent of maternal deaths.
- Seventy-two million children, 56 percent of whom are girls, remain out of school around the world.*
- Five thousand children die every day from severe diarrhea—the number-one cause of death in children under the age of five.

Every night they gather and sing. For an hour before bedtime the orphans on the other side of the hedge sing praise songs to God. There are sixty orphans living in the orphanage next to our guesthouse in Litien, Kenya.

Walking back to my room, I am stopped in my tracks by the perfectly pitched, hauntingly beautiful voices of children. They sing in Swahili and in English. The volume is sometimes loud and boisterous and joyful. At times the children sing with a peaceful quiet, full of reverence. It is pitch-dark on this far-flung hillside in Kenya. I stand alone, wishing the mesmerizing music would stop. *What is this ache in my heart?* It feels almost too much, as if it might crack something foundational in me, something I am quite sure I still need intact. Yet I linger, unable to leave it and shut it out. I stare at the hedge that separates us and listen.

I try to remind myself I am simply having a typical response to being confronted by outrageous poverty and inequality. I have tried to categorize it, explain it, critique

* First two statistics found at www.one.org.

it and process it with the other members on my team. Yet my heart is causing me trouble. This is not the first time I have seen firsthand the staggering reality of extreme poverty and the wildly disparaging gap between America and the developing world, but it something I never get used to.

The past few days I have not been able to stop the frantic tape in my head playing over and over, asking, *Where is God? How can He endure this kind of human suffering? Where is the justice? Where is relief and healing and clean water? Why should our quality of life depend so much on where we're born?*

Last night I had a dream.

I am in a quiet African village in which the people are eking out an impoverished existence. I am following a man. I mysteriously understand he is a God figure. He is walking in front of me, leading me down the red clay roads. I stumble on the rocky terrain and do my best to keep up with him. He does not speak, a lone figure on the dirty, rough roads. Silently he begins to point things out to me. I watch as he points down an alley. I follow as he points into this house, at that field, toward a distant well. We continue to walk—it seems endlessly—as he purposefully points the way.

Even while still dreaming, a realization comes to me. *He can do something.*

I am filled with an aching hope. Alone I can do nothing or even begin to bring relief to the immense suffering I have seen. I can do nothing to stop the onslaught of AIDS, the exploitation of women and children, the stupid poverty. In this dream I come to terms with my helplessness. By myself I *am* helpless, but I'm not here by myself. I am not alone—in Africa, in the world, or in my generation with all its troubles—God is here.

I reflect on this dream as the orphans over the hedge finish their nightly praise songs to God. I turn to enter the guesthouse where the team is staying. Flipping on the light in the small kitchen, I stand still, giving the roaches and mice time to jump off the counter and scurry across the cement floor. For the first few days, we tried vigilantly to keep the vermin off our food supply, but we soon gave up. How quickly you learn to accept things it seems you cannot control in this strange place. I boil water to make a cup of tea and cannot keep my mind from reflecting on my visit to the orphanage yesterday.

Eight white buildings surround a yard in a square. As we make our way across the compound, I look into the doorless dwellings. The floors of the bunkhouses are cement, and the bunk beds inside them hold thin, mostly bare mattresses except for an occasional blanket. I pause at one door, noticing I see no personal belongings. As I continue on my way I almost run into an emaciated cow lumbering and grazing on the anemic grass lawn.

My mother's heart is aching terribly, and I stepped foot in this orphanage only three minutes ago. Already, I see my three-year-old in a child holding an older boy's hand, my six-year-old daughter giggling with her hand over her mouth, and my ten-year-old son running like a madman, playfully hitting a friend and dodging retribution as he heads toward the multipurpose room where the children are gathering.

In the meeting hall, the children sit in rows on benches, their ill-fitting uniforms stained and ripped. I want to scrub them all down, head to toe, then get them some decent clothes and a good meal. My heart and mind are not happy with this moment and desperately want to slip away to a place where they do not have to deal with this—the impossible longing to give a mother's care to every needy child in the world.

After greeting us, the children sing. It is a gospel song in English, "In paradise, everything is gonna be all right. In Paradise everything is gonna be okay, okay, okay." As the children sing, they sway back and forth in perfect unison. Back and forth. Back and forth. Everything is going to be okay, left, okay, right, okay, left. Hypnotic, dull eyes, no smiles. Okay, left, okay, right, okay, left.

Disconcertingly, the swaying speaks to me of self-comfort, self-soothing. How a mother might gather her baby in her arms, rocking and cooing, "It'll be okay, sweetie. It'll be okay." Yet this is an entire room of motherless children soothing themselves.

Can a heart break into a million pieces for the millionth time?

Letting a tear fall down my cheek, I wonder, *Are they going to be okay? What is to become of them? What will their lives look like in two years, five years, ten years? As my children are preparing for college and high school proms, will these children have incurable diseases or abusive husbands? Will they have enough food?*

I sip my tea, thankful for creature comforts. Hugging the mug, I put my head back on the ratty cushion of the guesthouse couch. I reflect on this idea that in paradise, everything will be all right. I close my eyes and shake my head in frustration. This kind of theology doesn't cut it for me.

Of course, I believe everything will be made right and all of creation will be redeemed in paradise. When God created the world he said, "It is good." I do not believe God starts over in heaven with a whole new template of creation. This creation, this world, is *good,* and everything good in creation—the beauty of nature, every act of kindness, every gesture of humility and gratitude, every sacrificial offering and deed that builds up the church—all these and more will somehow, mysteriously, be continued into the next age. I do not believe when we die we are simply whisked up to heaven to sit on a cloud somewhere. This journey of faith, this world, and each of us—including the orphans over the hedge—we're all going somewhere far more dynamic and meaningful.

I believe this is why God works in the world. He loves this world and he will bring healing. He will make everything right. It is the whole point of the biblical story, that in Jesus's death and resurrection, God broke into humanity and started the world on the course toward full healing.

It is my thinking—and we pray together as Christians—"Thy kingdom come, Thy will be done [on] earth, as it is in heaven" (Matt. 6:9–10, KJV). Jesus himself taught us to pray this way. Jesus didn't say, "Sorry, folks, you'll just have to wait until you get to heaven or until I return for me to work in the world."

Emotionally, psychologically, I understand the temptation to think this way. How quickly did I give up fighting the roaches and mice in my food? It can seem too much. Too overwhelming. What can we really do? If powerful governments and multiple generations before us have not been able to arrest deadly disease, extreme poverty, and the suffering of innocent people, who are we to think we can do any better? I get it, but this acceptance of suffering is not what Jesus taught and it is not God's plan for his creation.

One of my favorite theologians, N. T. Wright, teaches that human beings reflect the image of God, and God intends this reflection of himself to be present in our world, here and now. He has enlisted us to act on his behalf in the project of healing creation and building his kingdom. Because Jesus brought the reality of this healed world through his resurrection, not only is acting on behalf of justice and compassion a way in which we seek God; it is also how we reflect God to a suffering world and build for the kingdom. Wright explains, "You are not planting roses in a garden that's about to be dug up for a building site. You are—strange though it may seem, almost as hard to believe as the resurrection itself—accomplishing something that will become in due course part of God's new world."

Imagine a father and child in the garage, working on building something together. The father knows the plan and could certainly build it himself, but he delights to have his small child with him. He hands the small child a hammer and some nails and some simple instructions. The child does not fully understand the entire project or how it will come together, but she happily starts banging and hammering. The child certainly helps the father, but it is only because the father equipped her. The father delights in including the child because he loves the child and longs to see her participate, but the father alone knows the plan.

First Corinthians 15:58 says, "Always give yourselves fully to the work of the Lord, because you know that your labor in the Lord is not in vain." Ultimately, in paradise, not only does the Father know the plan, but he alone transforms and redeems the whole project. He will "make all things new." Yet we are still called to participate in the healing of creation—somehow our efforts impact the future, the overall plan, and carry over into paradise.

N. T. Wright explains, "What we do in the Lord in 'not in vain' and that is the mandate we need for every act of justice and mercy, every program of ecology, every effort to reflect God's wise stewardly image into his creation." Creation is to be redeemed. God declared the whole project "very good." This challenges me with the idea of what am I to do in this in-between time—between the resurrection of Jesus and when God makes all things new? As a woman in the church, am I called to just wait in my comfortable life, feeling somewhat bad about the suffering in the world, or am I to work to bring the kingdom of heaven here and now?

CHAPTER FOUR

DOES GOD GET WHAT GOD WANTS?

Overview by Rob Bell

Some of the earliest seeds of the book came out of the content of this chapter. Jesus talks about the renewal of *all things;* Paul talks about the reconciliation of *all things;* and Peter talks about the restoration of *all things*. I remember, years ago, looking up that Greek phrase in the New Testament, and it is translated, well, literally: "all things." I had assumed there was some sort of caveat, some nuance: "Yes, in English it says 'all things,' but it actually is something else, you know. It actually means all the good people, all the religious people, all the Jesus people, all the people who are saved, reborn, redeemed." But, no, the phrase "all things" was pretty much the most inclusive, wide, embracing term you could use.

Why does this theme keep coming up, that God has some intent involving "all things"?

The question I'm trying to raise in the chapter is this: Is the thing that God is up to in the world through Jesus going to be smaller or bigger than our imagination? Is it going to shrink, or is it going to be something more expansive than we first thought? What direction is God's work going in the world? Is it getting smaller or is it getting bigger? If you're a person who is serious about Jesus or faith or you want to know God, then perhaps, as a matter of course, we should always build in a sense of increasing expectations: "Whatever this is, it's going to go beyond whatever I currently comprehend it to be." That is how God works. He goes before us and beyond us. My hope in this chapter is that the questions it raises and the scriptures it takes you through leave you with the sense of, "There may be way more going on here than I first realized."

Going Deeper by David Vanderveen

There is a long list of Old and New Testament verses that reflect God's deep desire to restore and redeem all people from all nations. If there is a constant theme in the Bible, it is that God will be united and reconciled with all people.

"Does God fail?" is another way to ask the title question of chapter 4. "Is history tragic?" is a related question Rob asks in relation to statements that some Christian churches make about the vast bulk of humanity being condemned to hell.

Many people choose to build lives, habits, and patterns that pursue a life in opposition to God. As people continue down these paths in this life and in the next, is it possible that the image of God in each of us could be erased? Is it also possible that people who reject God in this life have another chance or series of chances to accept God later? Maybe after they've experienced the fullness, the ultimate expression of their addictions, violence, pride, and other evil choices that separate them from God?

Many church fathers believed that God would ultimately restore everything. Restoration, renewal, and return are the great stories Jesus told and are the crux of Israel's story. God permanently turning his back on his people is never part of that story. Many serious disciples of Jesus believe that no one could resist God's pursuit forever.

Ultimately, no one knows the answer. We are all speculating based on our understanding of the texts we have. Knowing the nature of God, we have to believe that his story about the ultimate trajectory of history has to be the best possible story there is. Having different speculations about how it all ends doesn't make one Christian better than another.

What we do read is that the big story of God's love demands freedom and is permeated with God's love. Other Christians' ideas about God's story should not be our focus. Our primary concern should be to dig as deeply as we can into what God's story is.

Bible Study: "All Things"

Have you ever thought about the frequency and consistency with which the idea of "everything" or "everyone" is emphasized in scripture? Throughout both Testaments, whether the historical narratives, the wisdom literature, the prophets, Gospels, letters and (especially) Revelation, "everything" is simply "everywhere." A brief survey of some seminal passages, noted below, bear this out.

> All the ends of the earth
> will remember and turn to the LORD,
> and all the families of the nations
> will bow down before him,
> for dominion belongs to the LORD
> and he rules over the nations.
> All the rich of the earth will feast and worship;
> all who go down to the dust will kneel before
> him—
> those who cannot keep themselves alive.
> (Ps. 22:27–29)

> The earth is the LORD's, and everything in it,
> the world, and all who live in it. (Ps. 24:1)

> You who answer prayer,
> to you all people will come. . . .
> You answer us with awesome and righteous
> deeds,
> God our Savior,
> the hope of all the ends of the earth
> and of the farthest seas. (Ps. 65:2, 5)

The Lord is good to all;
he has compassion on all he has made. . . .
Your kingdom is an everlasting kingdom,
and your dominion endures through all generations.
The Lord is trustworthy in all he promises
and faithful in all he does. . . .
You open your hand
and satisfy the desires of every living thing.
The Lord is righteous in all his ways
and faithful in all he does. (Ps. 145: 9, 13, 16–17)

The Lord will lay bare his holy arm
in the sight of all the nations,
and all the ends of the earth will see
the salvation of our God. (Isa. 52:10)

Through him all things were made; without him nothing was made that has been made. (John 1:3)

For this reason I kneel before the Father, from whom every family in heaven and on earth derives its name. (Eph. 3:14–15)

"Who has ever given to God,
that God should repay them?"
For from him and through him and to him are all things.
To him be the glory forever! Amen. (Rom. 11:35–36)

> At the name of Jesus every knee should bow,
> in heaven and on earth and under the earth.
> (Phil. 2:10)

Then I saw "a new heaven and a new earth," for the first heaven and the first earth had passed away, and there was no longer any sea. I saw the Holy City, the new Jerusalem, coming down out of heaven from God, prepared as a bride beautifully dressed for her husband. And I heard a loud voice from the throne saying, "Look! God's dwelling place is now among the people, and he will dwell with them. They will be his people, and God himself will be with them and be their God. 'He will wipe every tear from their eyes. There will be no more death' or mourning or crying or pain, for the old order of things has passed away."

He who was seated on the throne said, "I am making everything new!" Then he said, "Write this down, for these words are trustworthy and true." (Rev. 21:1–5)

Discussion Questions

1. What do you think it means in 1 Timothy 2:4 that "God wants all people to be saved and to come to a knowledge of the truth"? Do you think God will fail or succeed in this desire?

2. As Rob shows, the Bible does not spell out all the details of what happens after we die. What might be God's purposes for not explaining everything and, instead, promising that we will be "surprised"? Why do you think various church traditions have spelled out exactly what will happen?
3. In the stories we read in the Bible, does God give up or continue pursuit? Does there seem to be a limit to the number of tries? What is God willing to give up to bring people back, to restore them?
4. Do you think an all-powerful loving God would allow the vast majority of human beings who have ever lived to suffer eternally? Why or why not?
5. Why is the freedom to choose fundamental to love?
6. In the Apostles' Creed, we confess that Jesus "descended into hell." What do you think this means? Why do orthodox Christians believe that Christ descended into hell? What do you think he did there?
7. Rob quotes many Bible passages that say God will ultimately restore everything and everybody. How do we reconcile these passages with those that talk about judgment and separation?
8. How we think of what happens at the end of the age tells a different story. Which story of how everything ends sounds the most credible to you? How do the different stories change how we think of the central character, God? Which story seems to fit better with the nature of God?

9. If God ultimately saves everybody, how do we deal with those who continue to choose evil? How do you think God deals with these people?
10. Near the end of the chapter, Rob asks whether all will be saved or some will "perish apart from God forever" and goes on to claim we do not need to resolve or answer this question. What do you think of his position? Do you think this question can be resolved? How?

READING **THE SECRET**

BY PETER ROLLINS

We can debate new models and paradigms for understanding God and even discover that we have glimpsed a deeper and wider vision of who we worship. But humans have the power (and tendency) to turn each new life-giving perspective into an idol, one we can then use as a cudgel to attack those who don't agree with us. When it comes to understanding God, a degree of humility must be our constant companion and we must accept that our understanding will never be complete. This balance between the wisdom of seeking to understand God and the wisdom of reticence in declaring God "understood" is what Peter Rollins gets at in "The Secret," taken from his book How (Not) to Speak of God *(Paraclete).*

Looking over what I have written, I find myself wondering once more why I have chosen the subject of God. After all, this area must be among the most difficult and dangerous of them all. So much ink has been spent in writing of God and so much blood has been spilled in the name of God that I shudder each time I think about writing on the subject. Because of this concern I have often found myself drawn to the sentiment expressed by the philosopher Ludwig Wittgenstein in the final sentence of his influential *Tractatus Logico-Philosophicus:*

> What we cannot speak about we must pass over in silence.

Time and again I have found great wisdom in this phrase, and yet I have not left these pages blank. Perhaps part of the reason why I find myself unable to stay silent derives from the fact that long before I ever came across this sentiment, I had become deeply involved with the evangelical charismatic movement. Here I learned a very different type of wisdom, one that I have never been able to shake. In short it was this:

> God is the one subject of whom we must never stop speaking.

At first these two approaches seemed like oil and water, yet I could not completely reject either. When the philosophical subtlety of the former gained power, I would find myself tempted toward a mystical humanism; and when the passion of the latter gained a stronger grip, I started a slide in the direction of religious fundamentalism.

Yet in the midst of this tug of war, I began to feel that these positions need not be enemies. The more I reflected upon the depth of these perspectives, the more I began to suspect that, far from being utterly foreign to each other, there was a way in which they could inform and enrich each other. More than this, I began to suspect that such a dialogue between these two positions not only could be personally liberating but also could unleash an approach to faith that might help to revitalize the Western church.

Yet the question remained as to what this dialogue would look like, for each time I reflected on the positions, I was struck by their seemingly exclusive and all-embracing nature. While Wittgenstein's God was an unbreakable secret that could not be shared, to contemporary evangelicals God was one who had broken this secrecy and thus needed to be shared.

Each time I returned to the horns of this dilemma, I found myself drawn to the Christian mystics (such as Meister Eckhart), for although they did not embrace total silence, they balked at the presumption of those who would seek to colonize the name "God" with concepts. Instead of viewing the unspeakable as that which brings all language to a halt, they realized that the unspeakable was precisely the place where the most inspiring language began. This God whose name was above every name gave birth not to a poverty of words, but to an excess of them. And so they wrote elegantly concerning the limits of writing and spoke eloquently about the brutality of words. By speaking with wounded words of their wounded Christ, these mystics helped to develop not a distinct religious tradition, but rather a way of engaging with and understanding already existing religious traditions: seeing them as a loving response to God rather than a way of defining God.

In these often overlooked writings I discovered a way to embrace both the wisdom of those who would say that God is unspeakable and must therefore be passed over in silence, and the wisdom of those who would say that God can, and must, be expressed. The union can be articulated like this:

> That which we cannot speak of is the one thing about whom and to whom we must never stop speaking.

For the mystic God was neither an unspeakable secret to be passed over in silence, nor a dissipated secret that had been laid bare in revelation. Rather, the mystic approached God as a secret which one was compelled to share, yet which retained its secrecy.

By the late medieval period this perspective was largely drowned out by the approach of theologians such as Duns Scotus, and it remained on the sidelines of faith throughout modernity (I am thinking here primarily of the influence of Cartesian thought). Even today, when I looked around, it seemed that the mystical approach was being either ignored by the wider Christian community or viewed as a private practice to be engaged in during remote weekend retreats. The only people who seemed to be taking this subject seriously were the supposedly nihilistic postmodern philosophers. Yet the more I studied this discourse, the more I returned to the view that this lost language was among the most stunning, sophisticated and simple ways of approaching faith. It became clear to me that for the Western church to prosper in the twenty-first century, it needed to engage with this ancient language.

READING

WHAT IS ETERNAL LIFE?

BY POPE BENEDICT XVI

There are a variety of orthodox Christian opinions about what the term "eternal life" means, particularly as it relates to life after death. Some of the simpler ones interpret eternal life to mean a continuation after death of our experience of time and life as we experience them now—a linear experience of time with a past, present, and future. Pope Benedict XVI, in his recent encyclical Spe Salvi, *discusses a historical Christian position on eternal life as a fullness of experience outside of time or, as he says at the end of Section 12, "the supreme moment of satisfaction, in which totality embraces us and we embrace totality." If we are to contemplate eternity, we need richer and deeper categories for understanding time and our life after death, as Pope Benedict demonstrates.*

The question arises: do we really want this—to live eternally? Perhaps many people reject the faith today simply because they do not find the prospect of eternal life attractive. What they desire is not eternal life at all, but this present life, for which faith in eternal life seems something of an impediment. To continue living forever—endlessly—appears more like a curse than a gift. Death, admittedly, one would wish to postpone for as long as possible. But to live always, without end—this, all things considered, can only be monotonous and ultimately unbearable. This is precisely the point made, for example, by

Saint Ambrose, one of the Church Fathers, in the funeral discourse for his deceased brother Satyrus: "Death was not part of nature; it became part of nature. God did not decree death from the beginning; he prescribed it as a remedy. Human life, because of sin . . . began to experience the burden of wretchedness in unremitting labor and unbearable sorrow. There had to be a limit to its evils; death had to restore what life had forfeited. Without the assistance of grace, immortality is more of a burden than a blessing."* A little earlier, Ambrose had said: "Death is, then, no cause for mourning, for it is the cause of mankind's salvation."†

11. Whatever precisely Saint Ambrose may have meant by these words, it is true that to eliminate death or to postpone it more or less indefinitely would place the earth and humanity in an impossible situation, and even for the individual would bring no benefit. Obviously there is a contradiction in our attitude, which points to an inner contradiction in our very existence. On the one hand, we do not want to die; above all, those who love us do not want us to die. Yet, on the other hand, neither do we want to continue living indefinitely, nor was the earth created with that in view. So what do we really want? Our paradoxical attitude gives rise to a deeper question: what in fact is "life"? And what does "eternity" really mean? There are moments when it suddenly seems clear to us: yes, this is what true "life" is—this is what it should be like.

---

* *De excessu fratris sui Satyri,* II, 47: CSEL 73, 274.

† *De excessu fratris sui Satyri,* II, 46: *CSEL* 73, 273.

Besides, what we call "life" in our everyday language is not real "life" at all. Saint Augustine, in the extended letter on prayer which he addressed to Proba, a wealthy Roman widow and mother of three consuls, once wrote this: ultimately we want only one thing—"the blessed life," the life which is simply life, simply "happiness." In the final analysis, there is nothing else that we ask for in prayer. Our journey has no other goal—it is about this alone. But then Augustine also says: looking more closely, we have no idea what we ultimately desire, what we would really like. We do not know this reality at all; even in those moments when we think we can reach out and touch it, it eludes us. "We do not know what we should pray for as we ought," he says, quoting Saint Paul (Rom. 8:26). All we know is that it is not this. Yet in not knowing, we know that this reality must exist. "There is therefore in us a certain learned ignorance (*docta ignorantia*), so to speak," he writes. We do not know what we would really like; we do not know this "true life"; and yet we know that there must be something we do not know toward which we feel driven.*

12. I think that in this very precise and permanently valid way, Augustine is describing man's essential situation, the situation that gives rise to all his contradictions and hopes. In some way we want life itself, true life, untouched even by death; yet at the same time we do not know the thing toward which we feel driven. We cannot stop reaching out for it, and yet we know that all we can experience or accomplish is not what we yearn for. This unknown "thing"

* Cf. Ep. 130 *Ad Probam* 14, 25–15, 28: CSEL 44, 68–73.

is the true "hope" which drives us, and at the same time the fact that it is unknown is the cause of all forms of despair and also of all efforts, whether positive or destructive, directed toward worldly authenticity and human authenticity. The term "eternal life" is intended to give a name to this known "unknown." Inevitably it is an inadequate term that creates confusion. "Eternal," in fact, suggests to us the idea of something interminable, and this frightens us; "life" makes us think of the life that we know and love and do not want to lose, even though very often it brings more toil than satisfaction, so that while on the one hand we desire it, on the other hand we do not want it. To imagine ourselves outside the temporality that imprisons us and in some way to sense that eternity is not an unending succession of days in the calendar, but something more like the supreme moment of satisfaction, in which totality embraces us and we embrace totality—this we can only attempt. It would be like plunging into the ocean of infinite love, a moment in which time—the before and after—no longer exists. We can only attempt to grasp the idea that such a moment is life in the full sense, a plunging ever anew into the vastness of being, in which we are simply overwhelmed with joy. This is how Jesus expresses it in Saint John's Gospel: "I will see you again and your hearts will rejoice, and no one will take your joy from you" (16:22). We must think along these lines if we want to understand the object of Christian hope, to understand what it is that our faith, our being with Christ, leads us to expect.*

* Cf. *Catechism of the Catholic Church,* 1025.

CHAPTER FIVE

DYING TO LIVE

Overview by Rob Bell

At the heart of the Christian faith is the event in which a group of people insisted that their rabbi, their teacher, their leader, Jesus, was crucified and then a little while later reappeared to them. They were so insistent that this actually happened that they were willing to die for it. At the heart of the Christian faith was an event in history about which a group of people were willing to go to their deaths saying, "This happened."

Now, this death and resurrection, though it was a new idea, also wasn't a new idea, because death and resurrection, death and rebirth, are essentially built into the very nature of creation. Think of the seasons: things die or lie dormant and then come back to life in the spring. In this chapter, beginning with this historical event, what I'm interested in is your tapping into the truth of the cross all over the place. If death and rebirth are a pattern, a truth built into the very nature of the universe, then what does that mean for us to say yes to the cross and resurrection and enter into that pattern of death and rebirth ourselves, day after day, year after year? What does it mean to find ourselves dying in order to really live?

Going Deeper by David Vanderveen

For many people the symbol of the cross has become so familiar that it has lost its meaning. Can we get back to the radical message that early Christians were trying to communicate using the cross?

Some get nervous when we explore new language for what Jesus accomplished on the cross and in his resurrection. Many define faith precisely by how well we do not change the language. They often stifle and oppose attempts to make God's message stay vital and meaningful. This tension between a "stingy" orthodoxy and a "generous" orthodoxy is taken up in the included reading from Richard Mouw, the president of Fuller Theological Seminary, the largest seminary in the United States, from his blog written during the launch of *Love Wins.*

The goal is not changing the Christian story, but recapturing the vitality of the original one. The point early Christians were making is that Jesus, the divine flesh and blood, is where the life is. Jesus's death on the cross does bring us back into communion with God through its justification, redemption, reconciliation, and other metaphors, but the point is that it ultimately starts a new creation for all creation. It's bigger than us; it includes everyone; it is cosmic in scope and includes everything.

Rob looks at three big ideas with respect to death and life:

1. Death and resurrection were not a new idea—it is the circle of life that is evident throughout creation.
2. God is rescuing all creation, including people.
3. The cross and resurrection are personal and involve how every one of us lives every day. It is a way of life.

Jesus repeatedly spoke about death and resurrection and his longing for us to be a part of his new creation—the kingdom of God in this new age. If we will repent, renounce, and confess our old ways and let them die, his new life can spring forth in us. We can participate in Christ's new creation if we will let our sinful self die.

Glenn Parrish helps us explore the meaning of following Christ and the problem of the overfamiliarity of symbols in his essay on how God has used mysterious emissaries throughout the Bible—from Melchizedek to the Magi. Jesus repeatedly surprised his followers with who was in and who was out, from tax collectors and prostitutes to Romans and Gentiles. Each time his followers are surprised, he seems to say, "What is that to you? The feast is cosmic in scope. Will you come join us?"

And Donald Miller talks about how taking the initiative in doing the unexpected can be a way for the Holy Spirit to do his work—such as the time he set up a confessional on campus in order to confess the sins of the church to those who showed up.

Bible Study: The Metaphorical Riches of the Cross

If there is any symbol that is universally recognized, it is the cross, two pieces of wood intersecting at a ninety-degree angle at two-thirds of the height from the ground. Could it be any simpler? The reality is, no symbol has ever been so universally misunderstood or otherwise controversial. The New Testament depicts the cross, in all its gruesome simplicity and metaphysical complexity, through a spectrum of metaphors and teachings. As you read the passages below, don't dwell so much on how to reconcile all these different ways for understanding Jesus's work on the cross, but instead try to focus on the power of the new reality the writers discovered and experienced that caused them to reach for such rich and varied ways to describe it.

> Whoever does not take up their cross and follow me is not worthy of me. (Matt. 10:38)

> Carrying his own cross, he went out to the place of the Skull (which in Aramaic is called Golgotha). (John 19:17)

> This righteousness is given through faith in Jesus Christ to all who believe. There is no difference between Jew and Gentile, for all have sinned and fall short of the glory of God, and all are justified

freely by his grace through the redemption that came by Christ Jesus. God presented Christ as a sacrifice of atonement, through the shedding of his blood—to be received by faith. He did this to demonstrate his justice, because in his forbearance he had left the sins committed beforehand unpunished—he did it to demonstrate his justice at the present time, so as to be just and the one who justifies those who have faith in Jesus. (Rom. 3:22–26)

For Christ did not send me to baptize, but to preach the gospel—not with wisdom and eloquence, lest the cross of Christ be emptied of its power. For the message of the cross is foolishness to those who are perishing, but to us who are being saved it is the power of God. (1 Cor. 1:17–18)

The last enemy to be destroyed is death. For he "has put everything under his feet." Now when it says that "everything" has been put under him, it is clear that this does not include God himself, who put everything under Christ. When he has done this, then the Son himself will be made subject to him who put everything under him, so that God may be all in all. (1 Cor. 15:26–28)

For Christ's love compels us, because we are convinced that one died for all, and therefore all died. And he died for all, that those who live should no longer live for themselves but for him who died for them and was raised again. (2 Cor. 5:14–15)

Brothers and sisters, if I am still preaching circumcision, why am I still being persecuted? In that case the offense of the cross has been abolished. (Gal. 5:11)

May I never boast except in the cross of our Lord Jesus Christ, through which the world has been crucified to me, and I to the world. (Gal. 6:14)

His purpose was to create in himself one new humanity out of the two, thus making peace, and in one body to reconcile both of them to God through the cross, by which he put to death their hostility. (Eph. 2:15–16)

And being found in appearance as a human being,
he humbled himself
by becoming obedient to death—
even death on a cross! (Phil. 2:8)

For, as I have often told you before and now tell you again even with tears, many live as enemies of the cross of Christ. (Phil. 3:18)

For God was pleased to have all his fullness dwell in him, and through him to reconcile to himself all things, whether things on earth or things in heaven, by making peace through his blood, shed on the cross. (Col. 1:19–20)

He forgave us all our sins, having canceled the charge of our legal indebtedness, which stood against us and condemned us; he has taken it away, nailing it to the cross. And having disarmed the powers and authorities, he made a public spectacle of them, triumphing over them by the cross. (Col. 2:13–15)

He died for us so that, whether we are awake or asleep, we may live together with him. (1 Thess. 5:10)

But join with me in suffering for the gospel, by the power of God, who has saved us and called us to a holy life—not because of anything we have done but because of his own purpose and grace. This grace was given us in Christ Jesus before the beginning of time, but it has now been revealed through the appearing of our Savior, Christ Jesus, who has destroyed death and has brought life and immortality to light through the gospel. (2 Tim. 1:8–10)

When Christ came as high priest of the good things that are now already here, he went through the greater and more perfect tabernacle that is not made with human hands, that is to say, is not a part of this creation. He did not enter by means of the blood of goats and calves; but he entered the Most Holy Place once for all by his own blood, thus obtaining eternal redemption. The blood of

> goats and bulls and the ashes of a heifer sprinkled on those who are ceremonially unclean sanctify them so that they are outwardly clean. How much more, then, will the blood of Christ, who through the eternal Spirit offered himself unblemished to God, cleanse our consciences from acts that lead to death, so that we may serve the living God!
>
> For this reason Christ is the mediator of a new covenant, that those who are called may receive the promised eternal inheritance—now that he has died as a ransom to set them free from the sins committed under the first covenant. (Heb. 9:11–15)

> For the joy set before him he endured the cross, scorning its shame, and sat down at the right hand of the throne of God. (Heb. 12:2)

> For Christ also suffered once for sins, the righteous for the unrighteous, to bring you to God. He was put to death in the body but made alive in the Spirit. (1 Pet. 3:18)

Group Exercise: What Is the Gospel?

Sometimes words and symbols can become overfamiliar and lose their meaning and impact for us. To recapture some of the power of the gospel message, have your group construct a statement of what the gospel is without using the words "Jesus," "Christ," "Christian," "cross," "sacrifice," "sin," or any other word only those who have been to church would know.

Discussion Questions

1. When you think of Christ's "sacrifice" for us, what do you think was the actual transaction that occurred?
2. How would you describe to others what Jesus accomplished on the cross and how it affects us today?
3. How meaningful to you are some of the words the Bible uses to describe Jesus's work on the cross—"sacrifice," "atonement," "justification," "redemption," "victory"?
4. What do you think of Rob's argument that the metaphor of sacrifice was more relevant to people during the time of Christ and immediately after than it is today? Do you think the message that there was no further need for sacrifice could have been misunderstood or considered unsettling for early Christians?
5. On p. 129 of *Love Wins,* Rob states, "The point then, as it is now, is Jesus. The divine flesh and blood. He's where the life is." What does this mean? How does this change how we view the cross and Jesus's sacrifice?
6. How does Jesus's death and resurrection relate to the basic pattern of life, death, and rebirth we witness in all of life? Is the resurrection just for people or for all of creation?
7. Do you agree that we are in the first day of a new creation? Is John telling a story about God rescuing all of creation? What does that mean for us?

8. What comes after Christ's death? How has resurrection been a concept that sustains life throughout the universe? How was Christ's resurrection the same and different from other examples of life sustained through death?
9. How are the cross and resurrection personal? How do the cross and resurrection impact every one of us every day?
10. What changes if we accept a more "cosmic" or "grand" understanding of Jesus's accomplishments and goals?
11. What does the cross mean to you after reading this chapter? Has it changed or grown in its meaning?

READING
MELCHIZEDEK, THE MAGI, AND ISA AL-MASI
BY GLENN PARRISH

Jesus is the rock in the wilderness, and there are rocks everywhere to sustain us. Unfortunately, the name "Jesus" and words like "Christian" have so much political and social baggage these days that, when people experience Christ but have been abused in his name, they find other names for the source of all grace, peace, and love in the universe. Glenn Parrish is a professional in social and venture philanthropy with a background in youth ministry. His essay showcases just how surprisingly wide and expansive the saving work of Christ can be.

> Melchizedek was the king of Salem and a priest for God Most High. He met Abraham when Abraham was coming back after defeating the kings. When they met Melchizedek blessed Abraham. . . . No one knows who Melchizedek's father or mother was, where he came from, when he was born or when he died. (Heb. 7:1–3)

I've always been drawn to the odd details in stories and life that hint at the deeper stories that lie beyond the page. Existence strikes me sometimes as sacramental and other times just quirky, but almost always shot through with clues of something more, something deeper. Scripture is studded with these sorts of hints to the myriad of stories behind stories—God and whatever he is doing in relationship with creation stretching out infinitely beyond my knowledge.

So we stumble across Melchizedek appearing out of nowhere at the beginning of one of God's great, recorded stories of his relationship with human beings. He is described as "a priest for God Most High." He blesses Abraham and then is gone. We know nothing substantial about his life or about the origin and content of his relationship with God. He is a God-follower before the Hebrew scriptures were written, before Judaism, well before Jesus comes on the scene.

At the beginning of another of the great stories of God's relationship with human beings, Magi from the east appear, guided by God through dreams and astrology. They come from a far-off country to bless and to worship the Christ child. Then they too disappear, guided by God through a dream, slipping out of the clutches of that paranoid tyrant Herod the Great. We are again told very little about the content of their relationship with God, although somehow he speaks to them through the stars.

Who are these people? How do they worship? How are they "saved"?

Apparently God, through the scriptures, isn't all that concerned about explaining the details to us. Jesus speaks of having "other sheep that will listen to his voice," but what language that voice will speak, what cultures they come from, and where in space and time those sheep are is not explained to us. In these things we would do well to heed the admonition Jesus gives to Peter in their post-resurrection talk. After asking Peter three times, "Do you love me?" (echoing Peter's three-time denial of Jesus and restoring him to service), Jesus tells Peter how he will die. Noticing that the disciple John is following them, Peter asks Jesus what will happen to him. Jesus responds, "If I want him to remain alive until I return, what is that to you? You must follow me." Peter's inquiry into John's story, John's relationship with Jesus, and the plans Jesus has for him receives a pretty stinging rebuke: "What's that to you? You must follow me."

Through my work as a board member of a foundation that supports work with poor Muslim tribes in the Philippines, I have been exposed to consistent examples of how God just really doesn't seem to care what we think about the appropriate way to follow, love, and worship him. Every January we make the long journey to visit with the leaders of various projects we are supporting and hear more stories of Isa al-Masi (Jesus the Messiah) and his work. One project that we support founded a mosque in Mindanao filled with followers of Isa al-Masi who worship him in Islamic fashion and do not consider themselves "Christians."

Christianity has a bit of a bad name in Mindanao with Muslim tribal people. After World War II the Christian government encouraged Christians from the northern Philippines to migrate to Mindanao, where they were able to acquire tribal lands for next to nothing, pushing the tribes up farther into the mountains. The Christians prospered and the tribes got poorer. Fighting ensued.

Isa is undaunted here. We frequently hear stories of how he calls to Muslims in dreams and visions. And in

Isa's mosque, his followers keep working out what fits within their traditions and what needs to be adjusted so that they might authentically follow him as Muslims. Missionaries have a measuring system for different levels of "contextualization" of the gospel in these settings. The "Isa-Mosque" fits one of the deepest levels and generates controversy as to whether or not these people are "saved." What is that to me?

Three years ago we heard about an imam of a primitive Muslim tribe in the remote mountains of Mindanao who teaches from the Gospels because they are truer—they are easier to understand and more compelling than the Qur'an. I'm not sure what else is happening there, but the detail is compelling and makes me want to go back and hear more stories.

Two years ago we met Dann Pantojah, a hippy Mennonite pastor who founded Peacebuilders in Mindanao. Dann and Peacebuilders have played a remarkable role in reconciliation work between the warring Muslim and Communist separatist movements and the Filipino government. Dann travels to the most dangerous places in Mindanao to help bring peace in the name of Isa.

Dann is frequently confronted by Muslims about whether or not he is trying to convert them to Christianity. His response is simple and true: He does long for them to become followers of Isa, but his mission is in the name of Isa to help bring peace. The response to this approach has been twofold: (1) "You are a better Jihadist than we are because even though you know we could kill you, you have come to try and do good"; and (2) those with whom he has met have dreams and visions of Isa coming to them, calling them to follow on a remarkably consistent basis.

We have heard stories of Isa appearing to tribes-people in dreams and visions apart from the "work" of any missionaries. "A man in white came to us . . ."

The hints of this work of God are judiciously spread through the Qur'an too. Jesus (Isa in Arabic) is mentioned 25 times. His titles are numerous and lofty. Some of them: a word from God, Messiah ("anointed one"), rasul Allah (like Muhammad, 4:171; 5:75), a spirit from God, a sign to the worlds (21:91).

Five years ago we were speaking with Bishop Efram Tendaro, the head of the Philippine Evangelical Council of Churches, about the remarkable placement of Filipino overseas workers. In Saudi Arabia alone there were almost 900,000 Filipinos, many of whom were believers in Jesus. At that time there were around 100 secret house churches. Many of these workers serve as nannies. They are raising the children of Islam praying and serving as they do.

A month after returning from the Philippines I received a call from a friend who said that a man named Tass was coming to town and I should meet him. He was a Palestinian and believer in Jesus. He was looking for funding for reconciliation work in Palestine between Jews and Arabs. In my line of work I frequently take these types of meetings, but I was unprepared for the way this one would impact me.

Tass, his wife Karen, and I met for lunch and he told me his story. Born in Palestine, then raised in Saudi

Arabia, he took on the cause of the PLO (Palestine Liberation Organization). Tass become a sniper and, at one point, Arafat's chauffeur. He hated Jews, hated Christians, and had killed both.

Fast forward with Tass: two years after leaving the PLO he was living in the United States. Because Tass liked his life here and had married a non-Muslim, his family disowned him and cut him off from their wealth.

Starting as a busboy at a restaurant, he bootstrapped himself to where he was able to buy his own restaurant and develop a successful business. But still something bothered him—Tass began to experience a terrible and nameless spiritual distress. Finally this distress was so compelling that he fell down on his knees next to the table of one of his regular customers, his friend, and begged for help.

Tass and his friend drove together to his friend's house—on the way in the car his friend told Tass that he was going to have to learn to love a Jew. Tass said that he nearly leapt from the car at this statement, but he was in such distress he just went along. In his friend's living room as he was being prayed for, Tass had a vision of light in the middle of which he saw two hands clasped together as in prayer. He recognized those hands by the small tattoo where the thumb and forefinger intersected. They were the hands of his Filipino nanny who had helped raised him in Saudi Arabia.

This sort of thing gives me chills and makes me weep with joy at the chance to see the deeper story behind the story, the untamable redemptive power of Isa. What a wild confirmation of Christ's love that we had heard in the Philippines!

Today Tass and Karen carry on a redemptive and dangerous work serving Palestinians and working to reconcile Jews and Arabs all in the name of Jesus. And so it goes.

God seems to like the dramatic turn, the sudden rescue, the surprise ending.

There are deeper stories all around us. God's love for people through Christ is cosmic. Jesus's love seemingly transcends time, space, and our religious boxes. If God is anything, he is love. If God wants to craft a plan to rescue everyone, what is that to you? All Jesus asks is, "You follow me."

READING
STINGY ORTHODOXY OR GENEROUS ORTHODOXY?
BY RICHARD J. MOUW

On March 15, 2011, during the height of the debate over the launch of Love Wins, *Richard J. Mouw, the president of evangelicalism's largest seminary, Fuller Theological Seminary, in Pasadena, California, raised in his blog an intriguing perspective on what was really at stake. Are we honoring God more when our doctrine is stingy or when our doctrine is generous? These are not often put forth as criteria in adjudicating Christian debates, but they certainly communicate strongly to others what kind of God we are projecting to the world.*

I told the *USA Today* reporter that Rob Bell's newly released *Love Wins* is a fine book and that I basically agree with his theology. I knew that the book was being widely criticized for having crossed the theological bridge from evangelical orthodoxy into universalism. Not true, I told the reporter. Rob Bell is calling us away from a stingy orthodoxy to a generous orthodoxy.

Let me say it clearly: I am not a universalist. I believe hell as a condition in the afterlife is real, and that it will be occupied. I think Rob believes that too. But he is a creative communicator who likes to prod, and even tease us a bit theologically. Suppose, he likes to say, we go up to someone and tell them that God loves them and sent Jesus to die for their sins. Accept Jesus right now, we say, because if ten minutes from now you die without accepting this offer, God will punish you forever in the fires of hell. What kind of God are we presenting to the person? Suppose we told someone that their human father has a wonderful gift for them, offered out of love for them—and then we add that, by the way, if they reject the gift that same father will torment them as long as they live. What would we think of such a father? Good question, I think.

If I were given the assignment of writing a careful theological essay on "The Eschatology of Rob Bell," I would begin by laying out the basics of C. S. Lewis's perspective on heaven and hell. Lewis held that we are created for a relationship with God as human beings who bear the divine image. When we rebel against God and commit ourselves to evil ways, we move further away from this positive relationship with God—and, thereby, further and further away from our humanity. Our ultimate destiny, then, if we do not change directions, is to cease to be human: we end up as monsters who have chosen to live in an outer darkness, removed from God and from other humans.

So, here is Rob Bell: people who refuse a "vital connection with the living God" are given over to a "kind of life [that] is less and less connected with God" (*Love Wins,* p. 66). And this is no mere theoretical state of affairs, "because it is absolutely vital that we acknowledge that love, grace *and humanity* can be rejected" (my italics)—and if so, "God gives us what we want, and if that's hell, we can have it" (p. 72).

And I certainly do believe that some folks choose that hell. The Hitler types. The man who kidnaps young girls and sells them into sexual slavery. They are well on their way to hell, to becoming inhuman monsters. To be sure, as the hymn rightly reminds us: "The vilest offender who truly believes / that moment from Jesus a pardon receives." But for those who persist in their wicked ways, eternal separation is the natural outcome of all the choices they have made along the way.

In a book I wrote several years ago defending the basics of a Calvinist perspective, I told about an elderly rabbi friend who struck me as a very godly person. He would often write to tell me that he was praying for me and my family. When he died, I said, I held out the hope that when he saw Jesus he would acknowledge that it was Him all along, and that Jesus would welcome him into the heavenly realm.

Some folks zeroed in on that one story to condemn me as a heretic. I find their attitude puzzling. Maybe they think that folks like Rob Bell and me go too far in the direction of leniency, but what about folks who go in the other direction? I just received an angry e-mail from someone who pulled a comment out of something I wrote a few years ago in *Christianity Today*. A prominent evangelical had criticized those of us who have been in a sustained dialogue with Catholics for giving the impression that a person can be saved without having the right theology about justification by faith. My response to that: of course a person can be saved without having the right theology of justification by faith. A straightforward question: Did Mother Teresa go to hell? My guess is that she was a little confused about justification by faith alone. If you think that means she went to hell, I have only one response: shame on you.

Why don't folks who criticize Rob Bell for wanting to let too many people in also go after people like that who want to keep too many people out? Why are we rougher on salvific generosity than on salvific stinginess?

In August 2006, *Newsweek* did an extensive report on an interview with Billy Graham. Graham made it clear that he is still firmly confident that Jesus is the only way to salvation. When asked, though, about the destiny of "good Jews, Muslims, Buddhists, Hindus or secular people," Billy had this to say: "Those are decisions only the Lord will make. It would be foolish for me to speculate on who will be there and who won't. . . . I don't want to speculate about all that. I believe the love of God is absolute. He said he gave his son for the whole world, and I think he loves everybody regardless of what label they have."

Billy Graham is no universalist. But he has come to a theology of salvific generosity, a perspective that he combines with a passionate proclamation of the message that Jesus alone is the Way, the Truth and the Life. For me—and I am convinced for Rob Bell—it doesn't get any better than that!

READING
CONFESSION
BY DONALD MILLER

The Christian culture has been both a force for good and a force for evil, as human institutions are bound to be. Donald Miller, in this excerpt from his book Blue Like Jazz *(Nelson), writes about a unique experience at Reed College in Oregon in which Christian students confessed the sins of Christians to students during a party weekend on campus. The life that grew from those Christian confessions is a great example of the familiar becoming refreshingly unfamiliar and the new life that awaits if we will release our sins.*

Saturday evening at Ren Fayre is alive and fun. The sun goes down over campus, and shortly after dark they shoot fireworks over the tennis courts. Students lay themselves out on a hill and laugh and point in bleary-eyed fascination. The highlight of the evening is a glow opera that packs the amphitheater with students and friends. The opera is designed to enhance mushroom trips. The actors wear all black and carry colorful puppets and cutouts that come alive in the black light. Everybody oohs and aahs.

The party goes till nearly dawn, so though it was late, we started working the booth. We lit tiki torches and mounted them in the ground just outside the booth. Tony and Ivan were saying that I should go first, which I didn't want to do, but I played bold and got in the booth. I sat on a bucket and watched the ceiling and the smoke from my pipe gather in the dark corners like ghosts. I could hear the rave happening in the student center across campus. I was picturing all the dancers, the girls in white shirts moving through the black light, the guys with the turntables in the loft, the big screen with the swirling images and all that energy coming out of the speakers, pounding through everybody's bodies, getting everybody up and down, up and down. *Nobody is going to confess anything,* I thought. *Who wants to stop dancing to confess their sins?* And I realized that this was a bad idea, that none of this was God's idea. Nobody was going to get angry, but nobody was going to care very much either.

There is nothing irrelevant about Christian spirituality, I kept thinking. God, if He is even there, has no voice in this place. Everyone wants to have a conversation about truth, but there isn't any truth anymore. The only truth is what is cool, what is on television, what protest is going on on what block, and it doesn't matter the issue; it only matters who is going to be there and will there be a party later and can any of us feel like we are relevant while we are at the party. And in the middle of it we are like Mormons on bikes. I sat there wondering whether any of this was true, whether Christianity spiritually was even true at all. You never question the truth of something until you have to explain it to a skeptic. I didn't feel like explaining it very much. I didn't feel like being in the booth or wearing that stupid monk outfit. I wanted to go to the rave. Everybody in there was cool, and we're just religious.

I was going to tell Tony that I didn't want to do it when he opened the curtain and said we had our first customer.

"What's up, man?" Duder sat himself on the chair with a smile on his face. He told me my pipe smelled good.

"Thanks," I said. I asked him his name, and he said his name was Jake. I shook his hand because I didn't know what to do, really.

"So, what is this? I'm supposed to tell you all of the juicy gossip I did at Ren Fayre, right?" Jake said.

"No."

"Okay, then what? What's the game?" he said.

"Not really a game. More of a confession thing."

"You want me to confess my sins, right?"

"No, that's not what we're doing really."

"What's the deal, man? What's with the monk outfit?"

"Well, we are, well, a group of Christians here on campus, you know."

"I see. Strange place for Christians, but I am listening."

"Thanks," I told him. He was being very patient

"Anyway, there is this group of us, just a few of us who were thinking about the way Christians have sort of wronged people over time. You know, the Crusades, all that stuff . . ."

"Well, I doubt you personally were involved in any of that, man."

"No, I wasn't," I told him. "But the thing is, we are followers of Jesus. We believe that He is God and all, and He represented certain ideas that we have sort of not done a good job at representing. He has asked us to represent Him well, but it can be very hard."

"I see," Jake said.

"So there is this group of us on campus who wanted to confess to you."

"You are confessing to me!" Jake said with a laugh.

"Yeah. We are confessing to you. I mean, I am confessing to you."

"You're serious." His laugh turned to something of a straight face.

I told him I was. He looked at me and told me I didn't have to. I told him I did, and I felt very strongly in that moment that I was supposed to tell Jake that I was sorry about everything.

"What are you confessing?" he asked.

I shook my head and looked at the ground. "Everything," I told him.

"Explain," he said.

"There's a lot. I will keep it short," I started. "Jesus said to feed the poor and to heal the sick. I have never done very much about that. Jesus said to love those who persecute me. I tend to lash out, especially if I feel threatened, you know, if my ego gets threatened. Jesus did not mix his spirituality with his politics. I grew up doing that. It got in the way of the central message of Christ. I know that was wrong, and I know that a lot of people will not listen to the words of Christ because people like me, who know Him, carry our own agendas into the conversation rather than just relaying the message Christ wanted to get across. There's a lot more, you know."

"It's all right, man" Jake said very tenderly. His eyes were starting to water.

"Well," I said, clearing my throat, "I am sorry for all of that."

"I forgive you," Jake said. And he meant it.

"Thanks," I told him.

He sat there and looked at the floor, then into the fire of a candle. "It's really cool what you guys are doing," he said. "A lot of people need to hear this."

"Have we hurt a lot of people?" I asked him,

"You haven't hurt me. I just think it isn't very popular to be a Christian, you know. Especially at a place like this. I don't think too many people have been hurt. Most people just have a strong reaction to what they see on television. All these well-dressed preachers supporting the Republicans."

"That's not the whole picture," I said. "That's just television. I have friends who are giving their lives to feed the poor and defend the defenseless. They are doing it for Christ."

"You really believe in Jesus, don't you?" he asked me.

"Yes, I think I do. Most often I do. I have doubts at times, but mostly I believe in Him. It's like there is something in me that causes me to believe, and I can't explain it."

"You said earlier that there was a central message of Christ. I don't really want to become a Christian, you know, but what is that message?"

"The message is that humans sinned against God and God gave the world over to humankind, and that if somebody wants to be rescued out of that, if somebody for instance finds it all very empty, Christ will rescue them if they want; if they ask forgiveness for being a part of that rebellion, then God will forgive them."

"What's the deal with the cross?" Jake asked.

"God says the wages of sin is death," I told him. "And Jesus died so that none of us would have to. If we have faith in that, then we are Christians.

"That is why people wear crosses?" he asked.

"I guess. I think it is sort of fashionable. Some people believe that if they have a cross around their neck or tattooed on them or something, it has some sort of mystical power."

"Do you believe that?" Jake asked.

"No," I answered. I told him that I thought mystical power came through faith in Jesus.

"What do you believe about God?" I asked him.

"I don't know. I guess I didn't believe for a long time, you know. The science of it is so sketchy. I guess I believe in God though. I believe somebody is responsible for all of this, this world we live in. It is all very confusing."

"Jake, if you want to know God, you can. I am just saying if you ever want to call on Jesus, He will be there."

"Thanks, man. I believe that you mean that." His eyes were watering again. "This is cool what you guys are doing," he repeated. "I am going to tell my friends about this."

"I don't know whether to thank you for that or not," I laughed. "I have to sit here and confess all my crap."

He looked at me very seriously. "It's worth it," he said.

He shook my hand, and when he left the booth there was somebody else ready to get in. It went on like that for a couple of hours. I talked to about thirty people; and Tony took confessions on a picnic table outside the booth. Many people wanted to hug when we were done. All of the people who visited the booth were grateful and gracious. I was being changed through the process. I went in with doubts and came out believing so strongly in Jesus I was ready to die and be with Him. I think that night was the beginning of change for a lot of us.

CHAPTER SIX

THERE ARE ROCKS EVERYWHERE

Overview by Rob Bell

For the first Christians Jesus was a real historical figure. They talked about this rabbi who taught and healed and gathered a crowd, and then he was crucified and resurrected. But as Christians over the next few centuries reflected on his life and death, as they discussed them, and as they talked about Jesus in the larger framework of redemptive history—as in, "What is God up to in human history?"—they began to develop very compelling and sophisticated ways of talking about Jesus. They believed that Jesus wasn't *just* a Jewish rabbi; rather, in him there was something present, someone present, the very God of the universe. The apostle Paul wrote that Jesus holds all things together. They believed he was like the glue of the universe. For them, Jesus was somehow present in all of creation. One of the words they used for this was "mystery," that there is a divine life source, an energy that holds all things together, that came among us in flesh and blood as Jesus.

Now, if you talk like that, it's going to raise all sorts of questions, because for many people Jesus exists within the Christian religion, and everything else is essentially outside of Jesus or God or Spirit. But for the first Christians it was the exact opposite: everything was held together and sustained by the very life-giving power and energy of the God of the universe. And they called this life-giving energy the "Word" and said that with Jesus the "Word" took on flesh and blood. Now this has serious implications. I hope that after reading the chapter, you will be able to ask yourself these questions: What does it mean to believe that Jesus holds all things together? Where else is Jesus present? What does this say about religions, and the way in which religions, specifically the Christian religion, interacts with other religions? This Jesus, once again, raises all sorts of questions.

Going Deeper by David Vanderveen

There are many stories of people who experience God in odd places and inexplicable ways. In Exodus 17 God tells Moses to strike a rock in order to give water to the Israelites. We hear later in 1 Corinthians 10 that Paul believes that rock in the wilderness to be Christ, because Paul believed Jesus was everywhere throughout creation.

From Genesis to the New Testament, we repeatedly hear about the "Word" or the "Word of God" being a part of the creation of the world, becoming flesh among us and revealing himself to us in his fullness.

The big surprise for Jewish Christians at the time of Paul was that the secret that had been hidden from their ancestors was being made known. The big secret was that God had been creating this rescue plan throughout human history and that it extended to everyone, even the Gentiles.

Jack Heaslip, the Irish sage, offers us more of his wisdom in a short essay about how God revealed his secret plans to Paul and, through Paul, to all of us. In particular, he asks us to take the time to read Ephesians 3. Be prepared for a wild dream.

Rob talks about the difficulty and disruption of a Jesus that surprises us. He talks about a person being raised in a Christian community, with Christian education and constant Christian messages. Sometimes the constant familiarity can make it hard to really know and understand a Jesus who's bigger than our ideas of him.

Again we see the repeated themes of Jesus coming for everybody and all people. We see a Jesus who is bigger than one religion. Christ lives outside the boxes we build to contain him. Jesus's language about being the gateway can be confusing. Although Christ is clear that he is the only way to get to God, he doesn't say what the mechanism is that gets people in. There is a wide variety of explanations for the mechanism through Jesus's gateway, from very exclusionist claims to universalist claims to claims saying that how the mechanism works is as mysterious as Christ left it in his unsaying way. In a reading later in this section, Anne Lamott describes just how unusual and unique the path to meeting Jesus can be in her tale of conversion from her book *Traveling Mercies.*

Jesus matters if you want to get to life with God. God extends that doorway to everyone—it's wide open. When we say, "Jesus," we have to be careful to avoid defining Jesus as smaller than the life source of the universe.

Rob points out three key ideas around who Jesus is and how he's connecting heaven, hell, and everyone who has ever lived:

1. We shouldn't be surprised when people stumble upon him and don't even recognize him, like the Israelites and the rock. Christ is there for them wherever they are.
2. Although Jesus is clear that he is the only way to God, his message was constantly expanding to include everyone, from sinners to Samaritans to Gentiles.
3. It is not our role to make judgments about people's eternal destinies—we must respect the saving work that is Christ's alone.

We are all sustained by the saving work of Christ, whether we recognize it or not. He is living water for the thirsty, even when the thirsty are as clueless as the Israelites wandering in the desert—he still gives us water from the rock whether we know him or not.

Bible Study: The Cosmic Christ

We sometimes get too familiar with the various portraits of Jesus we see in movies or read about in books. But several passages in scripture reveal that Jesus is much more than a human with special powers. Read the passages below and consider how wide and deep Jesus's person is, let alone his presence and work in the world today. Try to read these verses as if you are reading them for the first time and list what you learn about Jesus.

> In the beginning was the Word, and the Word was with God, and the Word was God. He was with God in the beginning. Through him all things were made; without him nothing was made that has been made. In him was life, and that life was the light of all people. The light shines in the darkness, and the darkness has not overcome it. (John 1:1–5)

> The Son is the image of the invisible God, the firstborn over all creation. For in him all things were created: things in heaven and on earth, visible and invisible, whether thrones or powers or rulers or authorities; all things have been created through him and for him. He is before all things, and in him all things hold together. And he is the head of the body, the church; he is the beginning and the firstborn from among the dead, so that in everything he might have the supremacy. (Col. 1:15–18)

My goal is that they may be encouraged in heart and united in love, so that they may have the full riches of complete understanding, in order that they may know the mystery of God, namely, Christ, in whom are hidden all the treasures of wisdom and knowledge. (Col. 2:2–3)

When I saw him, I fell at his feet as though dead. Then he placed his right hand on me and said: "Do not be afraid. I am the First and the Last. I am the Living One; I was dead, and now look, I am alive for ever and ever! And I hold the keys of death and Hades." (Rev. 1:17–18)

To the angel of the church in Smyrna write: These are the words of him who is the First and the Last, who died and came to life again. . . .

To the angel of the church in Pergamum write: These are the words of him who has the sharp, double-edged sword. . . .

To the angel of the church in Thyatira write: These are the words of the Son of God, whose eyes are like blazing fire and whose feet are like burnished bronze. . . .

To the angel of the church in Sardis write: These are the words of him who holds the seven spirits of God and the seven stars. . . .

To the angel of the church in Philadelphia write: These are the words of him who is holy and true, who holds the key of David. What he opens no one can shut, and what he shuts no one can open. . . .

To the angel of the church in Laodicea write: These are the words of the Amen, the faithful and true witness, the ruler of God's creation. (Rev. 2:8, 12, 18; 3:1, 7, 14)

Group Exercise: Where Are the Rocks?

Sit in a circle. In turn, everyone in the group is to describe the most surprising way Jesus has shown up in their life. The goal is to showcase the creative ways Jesus works in people's lives and to remind everyone that Jesus is very much alive and well and active today.

Discussion Questions

1. When you hear stories of people experiencing Jesus or a divine presence, how do you react? Is your tendency to believe them or not? Have you experienced God directly in this way?
2. Read Exodus 17 and 1 Corinthians 10. Where does Paul get the idea that Jesus was the rock in the wilderness?
3. What do you think early Christians meant by the "Word of God" being revealed "in its fullness"? Who is the "Word of God" for? What kind of power does it have? What do you think "fullness" implies?

4. Which is larger, the universe or your concept of it? How much room do you leave the universe to surprise you? What does Rob mean when he says, "[Jesus] is as narrow as himself and as wide as the universe" (p. 155)?
5. In reading passages such as Ephesians 1 and 3, Romans 11 and 16, and Colossians 12, we learn many things about God's rescue operation for humanity—such as how it was planned from before the foundation of the world and moves forward to reconcile all things. When did God start his plan to rescue humankind? What was he rescuing people from and toward? When did he reveal it? To whom did he originally reveal it and to whom did he extend it?
6. Is Jesus bigger than Christianity? Did he come for one group of people or everyone? What do you think Paul means in Colossians 1:23 when he says that the gospel "has been proclaimed to every creature under heaven"?
7. How does seeing Jesus as above all religions and cultures change how we approach people of different religions and cultures?
8. Jesus says, "I am the way and the truth and the life. No one comes to the Father except through me" (John 14:6). How have you heard "through me" explained? What do you think it might mean?
9. In John 12:47 Jesus explains that he "did not come to judge the world, but to save the world." How do we

"judge the world"? How do we participate in saving the world?

10. Does everyone need to see and recognize Jesus in order to be sustained by him? With Rob's expanded view of Jesus, where might be some new places and ways we see Jesus at work today? How does Rob's view of Jesus change how we explain the gospel to others?

READING
PLAYING WITH ROCKS
BY JACK HEASLIP

If Jesus can be a rock that gushes water for Moses, he can be many more things than we ever imagined. In fact, we may have encountered Jesus many times in the past and never have known it—and we will definitely meet him more times in the future. It is exactly this openness to the creativity and unexpectedness of how Jesus meets us that has captivated Jack Heaslip, which he shares with us here.

Have you had a "road to Damascus experience"? Maybe not. But you will have heard the term? A massive change of heart, of direction, of lifestyle, of pretty well everything. The story was about Paul, who was at that time called Saul—just to complicate things. He was on his way to Damascus to arrest followers of the Way, who were followers of Jesus but not nicknamed "Christians" until later—just to complicate things further. Saul was confronted by a bright light and fell to the ground. Some people claim he fell from a horse, which would make for a greater fall and be more dramatic. He couldn't see anything, but heard a voice saying, "Saul, Saul, why are you out to get me?" Saul asked—politely—"Who are you, Master?" Jesus owned up to being himself and told Saul to go into Damascus, where he would get further instructions. Three days later the instructions came to him through a wary but obedient man called Ananias, who restored Saul's sight. Saul was baptized and immediately started to preach that Jesus was the Son of God (Acts 9).

A complete U-turn. A dynamic force for the kingdom of God was, in Paul, equipped, empowered and let loose.

If you have had such an experience, you will identify with Paul. If you haven't, you may well be skeptical. Maybe if you had fallen off a horse and heard a voice, you might have headed to the nearest A&E [emergency room] and missed the moment. Maybe when you hear such stories you feel a little threatened, jealous, envious.

The important things were not the road traveled, whether or not there was a horse involved, the loss of sight, the number of days without food and drink. The important thing was that Saul met with Jesus. He experienced him and was changed utterly.

That process might take three days, thirty-three days, or thirty-three years. That's not the point. There is no competition, no essential set pattern, no time scale, no list of necessary characters. Just meeting with Jesus and what that may do for you.

Most importantly, no one is excluded.

I know that—and it is one of the best things I know. I know it because Paul told me. And he told me what his life's work was. He told me, he told the church in Ephesus, he told everyone. You can read what he said in the Letter to the Ephesians. Especially clear is chapter 3 of that letter.

I take it seriously when a person like Paul says that something is his life's work. Among all the amazing things he did, he reckoned that there was a number-one purpose in his life. He tells us of God's plan, which had been kept as a secret and a mystery. This secret was not known even to the ancestors. Maybe it is kept from some of today's church, too.

I don't know about you, but I would be pleased if I spent time doing as Paul did. I'd be honored if I could share in his life's work.

So what is the secret? What is this mystery about?

> The mystery is that people who have never heard of God and those who have heard of him all their lives (what I've been calling outsiders and insiders) stand on the same ground before God. They get the same offer, same help, same promises in Christ Jesus. The Message is accessible and welcoming to everyone, across the board. (Eph. 3:6, MSG)

Now this blows apart the notion of God's people as a tiny elite, a spiritually upmarket minority.

It contradicts the idea of exclusivity. To be honest, the concept of an exclusive people is attractive. A special people, set aside, better than others, bound for heaven. It is attractive to me, to many in churches, to small groups of like minds, to perfectionists.

But not, it seems, to God!

Paul reveals God's desire to challenge us with inclusivity. Ouch!? This is so threatening—frightening even—to many of us.

But not, it seems, to God!

He, we're told, has no favorites. But we have! Favorites and dislikes. I remember a shocking incident where a church member pointedly inquired, "Who let her in?" The "her" referred to was a somewhat scruffy woman who had wandered in from the street!

Outsiders and insiders stand on the same ground before God!

This is not Paul's plan, or my plan, or your plan, or Rob Bell's plan.

This is God's plan.

Paul says it came to him as a sheer gift, God handling all the details.

But if it is God's plan, we need to listen. We need to be challenged. We need to be relieved. We need to be encouraged.

Outsiders and insiders stand on the same ground before God.

That is good news. And it is for us to share without fear or favor. We can join with Paul in bringing out into the open what God has been doing "in secret and behind the scenes all along."

Behind the scenes God's promises to Abraham were greater than Abraham could have imagined.

"All the families of the Earth will be blessed through you" (Gen. 12:3, MSG).

I wonder, how much did Jeremiah understand of the secret when he spoke God's words to Israel? "This is the brand-new covenant that I will make with Israel when the time comes, I will put my law within them—write it on their hearts!—and be their God. And they will be my people" (Jer. 31:33, MSG).

So what does Paul do about all this? He humbly "gets down on his knees" and prays for the church at Ephesus. He prays for you, he prays for me. Let's appropriate this wonderful prayer. Make it our own. Hear it prayed for us. Be encouraged and empowered by it. It has still got legs, still got vitality, still credible and powerful.

> My response is to get down on my knees before the Father, this magnificent Father who parcels out all heaven and earth. I ask him to strengthen you by his Spirit—not a brute strength but a glorious inner strength—that Christ will live in you as you open the door and invite him in. And I ask him that with both feet planted firmly on love, you'll be able to take in with all followers of Jesus the extravagant dimensions of Christ's love. Reach out and experience the breadth! Test its length! Plumb the depths! Rise to the heights! Live full lives, full in the fullness of God.
>
> God can do anything, you know—far more than you could ever imagine or guess or request in your wildest dreams! He does it not by pushing us around but by working within us, his Spirit deeply and gently within us. (Eph. 3:14–20, MSG)

Will we be able to take in the extravagant dimensions of Christ's love? We must try!

Jesus said, "I came so they can have real and eternal life, more and better life than they ever dreamed of" (John 10:10, MSG).

How sad when we replace God's wonderful vision with a shriveled, limited mockery of the life we were created to enjoy.

Listen to Paul's confidence for himself and for us: "God can do anything . . . far more than you could ever imagine or guess or request in your wildest dreams!"

God wants us to have the wildest of dreams! Can we imagine that?

Paul ends his prayer with a shout of praise:

Glory to God in the church!
Glory to God in the Messiah, in Jesus!
Glory down all generations!
Glory through all millennia! Oh, yes! (Eph. 3:21, MSG)

READING
ALL RIGHT. YOU CAN COME IN
BY ANNE LAMOTT

Some Christians spend a lot of time debating what it means to be saved and the steps you must go through to convert to Christianity. There are as many pathways to conversion as there are churches. It is often described as if people sit in a vacuum and objectively make a decision to accept Christ into their hearts. Some of the best conversion stories, from Jesus calling his disciples to Paul's vision on the road to Damascus to C. S. Lewis's experience and many more, seem more like a pursuit and surrender. Anne Lamott is the author of many books about faith. In Traveling Mercies *(Anchor), she describes her rather unorthodox conversion, which is as beautiful and true as they come.*

That April of 1984, in the midst of this experience, Pammy took a fourth sample to the lab, and it finally came back positive. I had published three books by then, but none of them had sold particularly well, and I did not have the money or wherewithal to have a baby. The father was someone I had just met, who was married, and no one I wanted a real baby with. So Pammy one evening took me in for the abortion, and I was sadder than I'd been since my father died, and when she brought me home that night, I went upstairs to my loft with a pint of Bushmills and some of the codeine a nurse had given me for pain. I drank until early dawn.

The next night I did it again, and the next night, although by then the pills were gone.

I didn't go to the flea market the week of my abortion. I stayed home, and smoked dope and got drunk, and tried to write a little, and went for slow walks along the salt marsh with Pammy. On the seventh night, though, very drunk and just about to take a sleeping pill, I discovered that I was bleeding heavily. It did not stop over the next hour. I was going through a pad every fifteen minutes, and I thought I should call a doctor or Pammy, but I was so disgusted that I had gotten so drunk one week after an abortion that I just couldn't wake someone up and ask for help. I kept on changing Kotex, and I got very sober quickly. Several hours later, the blood stopped flowing and I got in bed, shaky and sad and too wild to have another drink or take a sleeping pill. I had a cigarette and turned off the light. After a while, as I lay there, I became aware of someone with me, hunkered down in the corner, and I just assumed it was my father, whose presence I had felt over the years when I was frightened and alone. The feeling was so strong that I actually turned on the light for a moment to make sure no one was there—of course, there wasn't. But after a while, in the dark again, I knew beyond any doubt that it was Jesus. I felt him as surely as I feel my dog lying nearby as I write this.

And I was appalled. I thought about my life and my brilliant hilarious progressive friends, I thought about what everyone would think of me if I became a Christian, and it seemed an utterly impossible thing that simply could not be allowed to happen. I turned to the wall and said out loud, "I would rather die."

I felt him just sitting there on his haunches in the corner of my sleeping loft, watching me with patience and love, and I squinched my eyes shut, but that didn't help because that's not what I was seeing him with.

Finally I fell asleep, and in the morning, he was gone.

This experience spooked me badly, but I thought it was just an apparition, born of fear and self-loathing and booze and loss of blood. But then everywhere I went, I had the feeling that a little cat was following me, wanting me to reach down and pick it up, wanting me to open the door and let it in. But I knew what would happen: you let a cat in one time, give it milk, and then it stays forever. So I tried to keep one step ahead of it, slamming my houseboat door when I entered or left.

And one week later, when I went back to church, I was so hungover that I couldn't stand up for the songs, and this time I stayed for the sermon, which I just thought was ridiculous, like someone trying to convince me of the existence of extraterrestrials, but the last song was so deep and raw and pure that I could not escape. It was as if the people were singing in between the notes, weeping and joyful at the same time, and I felt like their voices or *something* was rocking me in its bosom, holding me like a scared kid, and I opened up to that feeling—and it washed over me.

I began to cry and left before the benediction, and I raced home and felt the little cat running along at my heels, and I walked down the dock past dozens of potted flowers, under a sky as blue as one of God's own dreams, and I opened the door to my houseboat, and I stood there a minute, and then I hung my head and said, "Fuck it: I quit." I took a long deep breath and said out loud, "All right. You can come in."

So this was my beautiful moment of conversion.

CHAPTER SEVEN

THE GOOD NEWS IS BETTER THAN THAT

Overview by Rob Bell

Everybody has a story they are living out. We all have something we believe about who we are, and what we're doing here, and where we're headed. And here's what I find really, really compelling. For a lot of people, when you talk about grace and love, when you talk about the gospel, they think it is kind of easy and squishy. It's like, "Oh, that's easy. Anybody can believe that." But if you actually listen to what Jesus says about grace and love, it's very difficult. We cling so tightly to our story and our identity, to who we've decided we are and where we come from and where we're headed, but Jesus is prying those stories out of our hands. Jesus is working to open our hands, so that we might begin to trust and live into a different story.

In this chapter I'd like to see you explore your own story, what you believe about yourself. Because what the gospel does is challenge that story; it disrupts it; the gospel ruptures our story and you are given a new and better story about who God insists you truly are. Jesus is interested in taking us into *that* story. But in order to go into that story, we have to let go of the old story. In this chapter, we'll work through a story Jesus told, looking to be confronted with any ways in which we're trusting a story that isn't that good. Because the good news is better than that.

Going Deeper by David Vanderveen

Jesus's parable in Luke 15 of the prodigal son is a story about two sons who have become separated from their father in different ways. Each must learn to trust the father's account of what their own story is rather than their own version of their story in order to accept the joy, peace, and love the father has for them.

Interestingly, heaven and hell are intertwined in this story. Heaven is the party. The party is happening, and it is up to us to return to the father and accept his gracious unfairness. In the father's world, neither son gets what he deserves; they are both offered much more than they can imagine or earn.

Many people hear stories about a God who will do anything for them on earth, but will torment them forever afterward if they don't say the right prayer before they die. That does not sound like a perfectly good and loving

God or one you can trust. That version of God is toxic. It is anathema to "good news." It is bad news.

Rob says, "Hell is refusing to trust." Our beliefs shape our lives, and the outcomes of those beliefs or lack of beliefs make life hellish. Rob makes a few important distinctions:

1. Rejecting God's grace and love sets us on a path of misery and hell. We should never confuse God's essence and love with the outcomes of rejecting that love.
2. The gospel isn't about getting into heaven; it's not a ticket to anything or a map to a destination. It is an invitation to enter into life with God and participate in that party, that joy, now. Limiting that view to a story about heaven and hell creates a world of scarcity and fear rather than abundance and joy.
3. We do not need to be rescued from God. God rescues us from death, sin, and destruction. A distorted understanding of this creates behaviors and cultures of fear, violence, and other consequences that do not fit in the kingdom of God.

The good news is better than the story that the father is a slave driver. We don't do things to earn his favor; we have it already. Our Father corrects that story. He says, "I never was like that." God doesn't demand our perfection, because we can't attain that. He requests our love. The older brother shows that even our sense of our goodness or our belief that we deserve God's grace, joy, and peace can separate us from our Father as easily as our bad behavior.

We have God's love all the time if we will accept God's story for us. Heaven and hell are all around us. We are free to choose the reality we want. If we will trust the story for us told by the God of the universe that we are loved, we can share in the truest story, the good news that is better than we can imagine.

Author Cathleen Falsani did just that, trusting God's story for her even when it so differed from the story she wanted for herself. In the next reading, she tells the grace-filled story of how a trip to Africa became a lesson in trusting in God's surprises and in God's story for her.

Bible Study: Telling the Right Story

The parable of the lost son (or the prodigal son, Luke 15:11–32) serves as a classic summation about the spectrum of emotions that can unfold within a single family with complicated personalities in a moment of crisis. The story captures the seminal elements of familial bonds, whether parent-to-offspring or between siblings. Emotions span the range from delight, to distain, to despair, to devotion, and ultimately, to the hope of reconciliation. More important, the parable serves to help readers expand and elevate their understanding of the nature of God. Read the version below, then take some time to explore the themes of how each of the main characters relates to the others.

There was a man who had two sons. The younger one said to his father, "Father, give me my share of the estate." So he divided his property between them.

Not long after that, the younger son got together all he had, set off for a distant country and there squandered his wealth in wild living. After he had spent everything, there was a severe famine in that whole country, and he began to be in need. So he went and hired himself out to a citizen of that country, who sent him to his fields to feed pigs. He longed to fill his stomach with the pods that the pigs were eating, but no one gave him anything.

When he came to his senses, he said, "How many of my father's hired servants have food to spare, and here I am starving to death! I will set out and go back to my father and say to him: Father, I have sinned against heaven and against you. I am no longer worthy to be called your son; make me like one of your hired servants." So he got up and went to his father.

But while he was still a long way off, his father saw him and was filled with compassion for him; he ran to his son, threw his arms around him and kissed him.

The son said to him, "Father, I have sinned against heaven and against you. I am no longer worthy to be called your son."

But the father said to his servants, "Quick! Bring the best robe and put it on him. Put a ring on his finger and sandals on his feet. Bring the fattened calf and kill it. Let's have a feast and celebrate. For this son of mine was dead and is alive again; he was lost and is found." So they began to celebrate.

Meanwhile, the older son was in the field. When he came near the house, he heard music and dancing. So he called one of the servants and asked him what was going on. "Your brother has come," he replied, "and your father has killed the fattened calf because he has him back safe and sound."

The older brother became angry and refused to go in. So his father went out and pleaded with him. But he answered his father, "Look! All these years I've been slaving for you and never disobeyed your orders. Yet you never gave me even a young goat so I could celebrate with my friends. But when this son of yours who has squandered your property with prostitutes comes home, you kill the fattened calf for him!"

"My son," the father said, "you are always with me, and everything I have is yours. But we had to celebrate and be glad, because this brother of yours was dead and is alive again; he was lost and is found."

Discussion Questions

1. What story do you tell yourself about yourself? What story do you think God is telling you about yourself? How do the stories differ?
2. Read Luke 15:11–32. How does the story that the younger son tells differ from the story that the father tells? If you were the younger son, which story would you trust? What might prevent you from trusting the father's story?
3. Read the story again, this time paying attention to how the older son's story differs from his father's. If you were the older son, which story would you trust? Why might trusting the father's story be difficult? Do you think it might be harder for the older son to trust his father's story than the younger son? Why or why not?
4. Rob points out that the father practices "profound unfairness." What does the phrase mean and how is it related to grace, love, and justice?
5. How does the gospel confront our story with God's story? Do you believe God is fundamentally for you or against you?
6. If you knew of a father who was loving and generous to some of his children, but threatened and even tortured others, what would you think of him? Could you see how you might trust and love this father? Do you think God is both a loving and gracious father

and an eternal tormentor? What would motivate people to embrace this understanding of God?

7. Have you ever found it difficult to love God? What roles do fear, uncertainty, and doubt play in your faith? What roles do you think they should play?
8. Rob argues that the gospel should not be about "entrance" (who gets in), but about "enjoyment" and "participation," which open us up to joy, happiness, and even throwing a good party. Does this describe the Christian communities you have known or experienced? What role has joy played in your Christian life?
9. Why do you think some people embrace a gospel of scarcity (where the focus is on getting to somewhere else and excluding others)? How is the gospel a story of abundance and joy? Think about people and communities who are living a gospel of scarcity versus people and communities living a gospel of abundance. Which seems more like heaven and which seems more like hell?
10. What stories do you have to let go of to enjoy heaven now?

READING
TRUSTING THE STORY GOD IS TELLING
BY CATHLEEN FALSANI

Love Wins *describes the heaven and hell around us and how both are possible, even in the same place, depending on what stories we embrace for our lives. In the parable of the prodigal son, we see a father who offers the best possible stories for the lives of his sons if they will trust him with those stories. Cathleen Falsani is an author and columnist who writes about religion in daily life. She has written extensively about her own surprising adoption of a young boy, Vasco, from Malawi a few years ago. What she describes below is how she, her husband, Maurice, and their son-to-be had to let go of their own stories to believe and trust in God's story for them. The surprising good news of the story is a stunning example of the grace that exists amid the heaven and hell all around us if we will submit our lives, our stories, to God.*

On my birthday, at the ripe old age of twenty-five, I had a mid-life crisis. I realized that I couldn't—and shouldn't—marry the perfectly lovely man I'd been dating for several years. It jarred me to think that I might never marry. Might never have children. Might spend my life as a jet-setting reporter, collecting rich, if unshared, memories. I told God, and myself, that I was okay with that.

But now that I'm forty, I look back on that moment and see how anemic my imagination was: the story God was writing for me was so much better than that.

By my twenty-seventh birthday, I had met, fallen in love, with and was engaged to my soul mate. Maurice was one of the two greatest surprises of my life. He wasn't what I expected the man God might have for me to join my life with to look like. He was older than me—by twenty years—divorced, with four older children. And he was a new believer, fresh and wide-eyed in his burgeoning faith. (I had given my life to Jesus as a ten-year-old. Didn't everyone?)

But Maurice was, in every way, perfect for me. In our fourteen years of marriage, God has proven to me and those closest to us how beautiful his choice of a mate was for me. Over and over and over again.

My husband opens my mind and heart in seemingly impossible ways. About six months into our married life, I remember having a mighty epiphany sitting in the car in the parking lot of a grocery store. I looked at my husband walking toward the car with a bag of produce and lobsters, which he'd bought to make dinner for my parents, and I felt almost overwhelmed by my love for him. And, in that moment, I experienced a sudden urge to have a child with him.

"I get it now," I thought. "Now I understand why people want to have children. I want to create a family with this man. I want to raise a little person who has his father's eyes and his remarkable heart."

There might as well have been a burning bush sitting next to me in the passenger seat, telling me I was meant to be a mother.

For the next nine years, Maurice and I hoped and tried to have a baby. But it didn't happen. We decided early on that we wouldn't obsess about becoming pregnant. We'd seen too many friends struggle mightily with infertility and become so consumed by it that it took a heavy toll on their marriage.

On my thirty-seventh birthday, I was still childless. My mother was thirty-seven when she had me, so passing that milestone gave me pause. Still, I was determined not to obsess and tried to rest in the knowledge that God had a plan for my life, and if it didn't involve a child—the desire of my heart—that would be okay too.

But it was the desire of my heart. A desire so deep and aching that I could feel it, like a pulled muscle.

Shortly after my birthday came and went, my husband and I departed on a holiday in Africa to celebrate our tenth anniversary. About a year before, we'd won a two-week trip to East Africa in a raffle. (Yes, really, a raffle.)

At the time, I was working on a book about grace—how God's unearnable gift shows up in fantastic and staggering ways when we least expect it. I figured that seeing Africa for the first time would be great fodder for the book, knowing that grace would indeed turn up, with jazz hands and in Technicolor.

The trip we won was to Kenya, Tanzania, and Zanzibar. While we were "in the neighborhood," we figured we'd add on a couple of days and fly to Malawi, the tiny, bean-shaped nation nestled between Tanzania, Zambia, and Mozambique, that is among the poorest in the world.

A few years earlier we'd given some money to an organization in Blantyre, Malawi, that works with street children. Malawi, like so many sub-Saharan African nations, has been ravaged by the AIDS pandemic. There are an estimated one million AIDS orphans in the tiny nation, and many of them end up living on the streets.

We landed in Blantyre on October 11, 2007, and spent the following day visiting with a couple dozen adolescent boys, most of them orphans, at a drop-in center run by the charity we'd donated to, an organization called, appropriately enough, Chisomo, a word that means "grace" in Malawi's predominant language, Chichewa.

Later that day, on the way back to our motel, a social worker from Chisomo asked if we'd mind making one more stop to meet one more boy. "He's just kind of special to me," our guide said.

I think back on that moment often, wondering what my life would be like if our response had been different. We could have said that we were tired, which we were, and wanted to head back to Pedro's Lodge to decompress with a beer.

But we didn't.

Thank God.

"Sure," we said. "We'd be happy to."

After a ten-minute drive toward the airport on the outskirts of Blantyre, our van pulled to the side of the road and we disembarked, following our guide down a muddy embankment toward a clutch of mud-and-wattle huts in a clearing a few yards away.

Our guide yelled something in Chichewa, and moments later a tiny boy emerged from one of the huts. He was a little wisp of a thing, maybe thirty pounds and the size of a scrawny American toddler. He had huge eyes and a decidedly regal countenance. A beautiful child. He walked toward us tentatively and climbed into the lap of our guide.

This was Vasco. He was about eight years old at the time, an AIDS orphan who had been living alone on the streets when our guide from Chisomo met him several months earlier. As is the custom in Malawi, Chisomo worked for months to find any living relative and eventually placed Vasco with his mother's one surviving sister, Esme, a woman about my age who looked twenty years my senior and had eight children and several grandchildren. They were a desperately poor family, but they took Vasco in and tried to provide for him as best they could.

A few minutes into our conversation with Esme and a few other extended family members, Vasco wandered over to me and, when I motioned to him that it was okay, sat down on my lap and leaned into my chest.

That's when I realized something was wrong.

Vasco's heart was beating so violently that his slender back was moving my body. I took a better look at him and noticed that he was sweating. It wasn't particularly hot out and he'd been sleeping when we arrived, not running around or playing. I looked at his eyes and saw that they were yellow and rheumy. He was panting, struggling to breathe.

"What's wrong with him?" I asked.

Vasco had a hole in his heart, he explained. The family didn't know much more than that, but they had taken him to a doctor once upon a time and had a chest X-ray. Esme asked one of the older children to fetch the film from her home, the largest of the huts in the family compound.

I held the X-ray up to the light and could see a large dark shadow where Vasco's heart should be. It cast a pall across two-thirds of his narrow chest.

My husband and I got as much information from Vasco's extended family as they had, but it was scant. Vasco's mother and father had died (presumably of AIDS) years before, and for a time he lived on the streets, begging for food and spare change.

My husband and I are journalists by trade, not physicians, but it was clear to both of us that Vasco was dying. He was in dire need of help in a place where there wasn't any help to be had. In the day we had left in Malawi, we tried our best to get someone to help Vasco, but no one was able, or, more honestly, no one was willing to do so. He was "just" a street kid. There were so many children who needed help. "We can only do so much," a senior social worker told us.

Sunday came. It was our day to depart. Once again, we gathered with Vasco and his extended family before heading down the road to the airport to catch our flight back to Kenya. I didn't want to leave. In truth, I just didn't want to leave Vasco. I wanted to tuck him into my carry-on duffle bag (he would have fit) and sneak him onto the plane. But I couldn't do that. I had to leave him behind.

As we left, I hugged Vasco tightly, told him that we'd see him again and that I loved him, which I did. I'm sure he couldn't understand me—he spoke no English—but I meant every word and hoped he got what I was feeling: that he was loved, that we cared, that we would do whatever we could to help him.

I'm not wealthy and I'm not a diplomat, but I am a writer. So I did the only thing I could: I told Vasco's story in the pages of the *Chicago Sun-Times;* I was a columnist at the paper at the time. My column ran on a Friday morning. By Saturday morning, three hospitals and a half dozen doctors had volunteered to fix Vasco's heart for free if we could get him to the States.

It took eighteen months—the longest eighteen months of my life—to get him to Chicago, but after many ups and downs, false starts, reams of red tape and the unbelievable kindness of dozens of strangers who donated time, money, and airfare, Vasco arrived at O'Hare International Airport on April 29, 2009. Open-heart surgery to repair the large ventricular septal defect—the hole—in his heart was scheduled for two weeks later.

While Vasco awaited surgery, undergoing a battery of tests and vaccinations, he stayed with my husband and me. Our intention was not to adopt Vasco. It was impossible, we were told. Malawi had a strict three-year in-country residency requirement before an adoption could even be considered. We simply wanted to fix his heart and save his life. Then he'd have to return to Malawi, where we hoped to set up a trust fund for him and enroll him in boarding school to make sure he was taken care of for the rest of his childhood.

That was our plan, but it wasn't the story God was writing. Two weeks after Vasco arrived in Chicago, on Mother's Day (because God has a sense of occasion), Vasco spiked a fever while we were in church. The next day we learned that he had a raging case of malaria, an all too common tropical disease in Malawi that had a two-week incubation period. If Vasco had fallen ill before he left for the States, he would not have been able to travel and, given his fragile health, likely would have died.

The malaria pushed Vasco's surgery back another six weeks, and during that time my husband and I got to know him better. Maurice and I fell head-over-heels in love with him. He was so bright and vibrant, with a marvelous sense of humor and a mighty spirit. Even as I had to carry him on my hip from place to place because he was too weak to walk, his soul was fierce. He loved life, people, new experiences. He wanted to live.

I've only met a few other people in my life who have the same ability to suck all the oxygen out of a room. People are drawn to him. Strangers come up and hug him, or just look at him and smile.

Vasco had open-heart surgery in early June 2009 at the Heart Institute for Children at Advocate Hope Children's Hospital outside Chicago. The operation was wildly successful. By the time surgeons wheeled him out of the operating room, his enlarged heart had already begun to shrink to a normal size. He recovered beautifully, emerging from general anesthesia a day earlier than doctors anticipated, smiling and full of life.

A few days after his surgery, as nurses were preparing to move him from intensive care to a regular hospital room, I looked up at the television nearby and saw a headline on one of the news channels that said the singer Madonna had been given permission to adopt her daughter Chifundo (Mercy) from Malawi.

Madonna's adoption journey was something I'd watched closely. A couple of years before, she'd adopted a boy named David Banda from an orphanage in northern Malawi, causing an international uproar. Some Malawians thought that she'd been able to bypass the country's residency requirement because of her wealth and celebrity. In 2008, when she sought to adopt a second child, Mercy, from an orphanage outside Blantyre, Vasco's hometown, the Malawian court denied her petition. Madonna, never one to walk away from a fight, appealed the lower court's decision. And in early June 2009, the Malawian high court ruled in her favor, approving Mercy's adoption.

I remember seeing the news and thinking, "I don't know what kind of court system they have in Malawi, but that sounds like case law to me."

Blessedly, the appeals ruling in Madonna's adoption of Mercy was, in fact, case law that opened the door for us to adopt Vasco. He didn't have to return to Malawi. He could stay with us and, if God and the courts were on our side, become our child.

Not long after Vasco was released from the hospital, we sat down with him in our living room and, with the help of a Malawian friend, told him that we would like to become his parents, that it would be the greatest honor to be his forever family, and that we loved him. But it was his choice. If he wanted to return to Malawi, we would help him do that and make sure he was taken care of in every way.

Vasco is a remarkably thoughtful person, with wisdom and grace well beyond his years. He thought for a few moments and then answered in Chichewa that yes, that would be just fine, he'd like us to be his parents, but wanted to be sure he could return to Malawi at some point to see his friends and family members there.

I'm not sure what Vasco thought his future would have been up until that moment. He still says very little about his life in Malawi before we met, some of the memories too painful for him to discuss.

Thinking back on that moment, I see that Vasco had to trust in the story that we saw unfolding for him, the story that God, the three of us believe, was writing. It was different from the one he had envisioned. It was better. The truth was more beautiful than anything any of us could have imagined.

For him. For us. For me.

Trusting in the beauty of that reality, in the grace of the true story, hasn't always been easy for Vasco. In his young life, he'd lost nearly everyone he loved. His mother, his father, his grandparents, several siblings. His life was nervous, unsafe, uncertain and unpredictable.

"My daddy died. My mommy died. My *gogo* (grandmother) died," he said to me a couple of years back. "Too many people die. Sometimes life in Malawi was very hard. And sad."

It took him many months to embrace the safety God had given him in my arms, in our family—blood and chosen—and in our unconditional love for him. At first, every time I left the house to run an errand, he'd panic that I would never return. Together, my husband and I and our beloved child learned to trust each other and the love God had given us for each other.

Henri Nouwen wrote, "Accepting love, forgiveness and healing is often harder than giving it." I clung to those words in May 2010 when the three of us boarded a flight to Malawi for Vasco's adoption hearing. The future, once again, felt dangerously uncertain. The court could deny our adoption petition. They could insist Vasco stay in Malawi. We might have to fight for him, relocate to Malawi, cause an international incident. We couldn't see the big picture, how the story would end. But God did.

The true story was this: on June 1, 2010, in a five-minute hearing at the high court of Malawi in Blantyre, a judge approved our adoption, citing the case of Madonna's daughter Mercy—mercy, come on!—as binding case law.

In what felt like the blink of an eye, Vasco was our son.

Forever.

Two weeks later, on a plane departing from the same airport in Blantyre, where I had to leave him behind three years before, my son—my beautiful son, my only child, the light of my life and joy of my soul—sat next to me, holding my hand and his father's hand across the aisle, as we took off together, headed home to California.

How improbable. How utterly miraculous. Staggering grace. Audacious lavish love. A happier happily-ever-after than I ever could have written myself.

Sometimes the truth is better than our imagination. It's truer than the impossible. We just need to believe it.

And that's the best story I know.

CHAPTER EIGHT

THE END IS HERE

Overview by Rob Bell

One simple idea is featured in this chapter—urgency. Jesus does not speak of a lazy, complacent, "I'll get around to it someday" kind of faith. He talks about a life that is available for every one of us right here, right now. We are invited to trust that our story has been retold and God really is that good and God's love really is for all of us. When we say no, when we harden our hearts, when we don't trust, when we close ourselves, there are consequences. As Jesus tells story after story, parable after parable, teaching after teaching, he keeps coming back to the urgency of *now.*

Sometimes people push back on this. They say, "Well, now, if you make it that easy, if you make God's love an all-around-us, ever-present sort of thing, then people are basically going to live however they want, and then right before they die, they'll make better choices." But that isn't the gospel. Any sort of authentic, real, true, beautiful response to the gospel will always lead to a heightened sense of awareness about this moment, right here, right now. Joy now, peace now, forgiveness now, reconciliation now, love now. The end is here, and Jesus insists that we can live right now in this love of God.

Going Deeper by David Vanderveen

The end of *Love Wins* is about trusting and embracing the new story that Jesus has for us.

Rob tells a story about his own childhood prayer for repentance and to accept Christ. He explains what that did to him and in him, that it was a life-changing experience that continues to shape his life today.

That the love of God is for all of us is the point of *Love Wins.* God's love is offered to us over and over and over again, yet history moves forward. We do not get the opportunity to go backward in time. This love can shape us into something greater than we can imagine if we will let it—or it will not do this work, if we don't let it.

To embrace transformation, we have to let go. We must have our own death and resurrection. We must leave behind our old selves and become something new.

Jesus's invitation is constant and it is urgent—it never ceases and it never decreases in its importance. Rob lists five parables or stories about people who avoided or failed to embrace the invitation to accept Jesus's love and transform themselves and what that meant in the new creation, how it left them out (see the Bible Study below). Our ideas define our choices, which define who we become. They matter more than we can possibly imagine.

But how these choices work themselves out remains a deep mystery. In "Do You Really Believe Anything *Happens* After You Die?" from his memoir *The Eyes of the Heart* (HarperOne), Frederick Buechner captures this mystery and our humble stance before it, while also demonstrating faithfulness.

Rob's concluding statement should not be summarized:

> Jesus passionately urges us to live like the end is
> here,
> now,
> today.
>
> Love is what God is,
> love is why Jesus came,
> and love is why he continues to come,
> year after year to person after person.
>
> Love is why I've written this book, and
> love is what I want to leave you with.
>
> May you experience this vast,
> expansive, infinite, indestructible love
> that has been yours all along.
> May you discover that this love is as wide
> as the sky and as small as the cracks in
> your heart no one else knows about.

And may you know,
deep in your bones,
that love wins.

Bible Study: Parables of Urgency

Jesus commonly employed storytelling, specifically the use of parables, to convey his most profound lessons about the movements of God and the principles of his kingdom. The parables below carry a strong element of urgency related to actions or nonactions of those living in real time, but which carry eternal consequences. Though simple and even rustic in their telling, Jesus's parables reveal the urgency of the "here and now" and how our choices shape eternal destinies.

The Parable of the Ten Virgins

> At that time the kingdom of heaven will be like ten virgins who took their lamps and went out to meet the bridegroom. Five of them were foolish and five were wise. The foolish ones took their lamps but did not take any oil with them. The wise, however, took oil in jars along with their lamps. The bridegroom was a long time in coming, and they all became drowsy and fell asleep.
>
> At midnight the cry rang out: "Here's the bridegroom! Come out to meet him!"
>
> Then all the virgins woke up and trimmed their lamps. The foolish ones said to the wise, "Give us some of your oil; our lamps are going out."

"No," they replied, "there may not be enough for both us and you. Instead, go to those who sell oil and buy some for yourselves."

But while they were on their way to buy the oil, the bridegroom arrived. The virgins who were ready went in with him to the wedding banquet. And the door was shut.

Later the others also came. "Sir! Sir!" they said. "Open the door for us!"

But he replied, "Truly I tell you, I don't know you."

Therefore keep watch, because you do not know the day or the hour. (Matt. 25:1–13)

The Parable of the Rich Fool

The ground of a certain rich man yielded an abundant harvest. He thought to himself, "What shall I do? I have no place to store my crops."

Then he said, "This is what I'll do. I will tear down my barns and build bigger ones, and there I will store my surplus grain. And I'll say to myself, 'You have plenty of grain laid up for many years. Take life easy; eat, drink and be merry.' "

But God said to him, "You fool! This very night your life will be demanded from you. Then who will get what you have prepared for yourself?"

This is how it will be with those who store up things for themselves but are not rich toward God. (Luke 12:16–21)

The Parables of the Hidden Treasure and the Pearl
The kingdom of heaven is like treasure hidden in a field. When a man found it, he hid it again, and then in his joy went and sold all he had and bought that field. (Matt. 13:44)

Again, the kingdom of heaven is like a merchant looking for fine pearls. When he found one of great value, he went away and sold everything he had and bought it. (Matt. 13:45–46)

Discussion Questions

1. Rob recalls the moment from his childhood when he decided to be a Christian. How have your early experiences of faith shaped your current faith life? What do you think of your earlier spiritual experiences today?
2. How are past experiences and earlier understandings about faith important? Why should they not be dismissed?
3. Why is trust, particularly the trust in a new story being told about us, a challenging concept to understand, absorb, and put into practice?
4. Why do we have to repent in order to be transformed? What specifically do you think you have to let go of to accept this change? Does that scare you? Do you trust God enough to let go and allow yourself to experience transformation?

5. How can an invitation be infinitely urgent? Why does Jesus repeatedly invite us to repent and accept his love? What kind of a process is the transformation of our hearts and lives? Does it happen once or repeatedly throughout our lives? How have you seen it work in others?
6. How does our spiritual outlook change when we think of God's invitation to us shifting from where we will go when we die to a relationship right here and now?
7. Why does Jesus think that the choices we make now matter so much? How might our choices today have a cosmic impact? If your heavenly life begins now, how might that change your life, your goals, your focus, and your everyday life?
8. Reread the excerpt from the end of the book reprinted above. How does this message about God's love for us fit with the teachings on heaven and hell in the book? Do you agree or disagree with these statements about God's love for you?
9. How have your views changed since reading *Love Wins*? What changes may result from reading the book?
10. Do you believe that "love wins"?

READING
DO YOU REALLY BELIEVE ANYTHING *HAPPENS* AFTER YOU DIE?
BY FREDERICK BUECHNER

Fredrick Buechner writes simple and beautiful prose that sheds light on the great mysteries of faith with profound honesty. In his memoir The Eyes of the Heart *(HarperOne), Buechner tells the stories of his family and friends and their own struggles with doubt, faith, and death. In the excerpts below, perhaps the authenticity of the author's doubt is what makes his resulting faith, belief, and prayer so sublime.*

My mother, the elder of Naya's two daughters, refused to talk about death the way she refused to talk about a great many other things. I remember telling her once that unless she started balancing her checkbook, she would go on overdrawing her account with disastrous results for the rest of eternity, and before I had much more than begun my lecture, she clapped her hands over her ears so she couldn't hear a syllable. She refused to even talk about people she loved who had died—Naya, for instance. It made her too sad, she said. Her New York apartment was full of photographs in silver frames, leather frames, Victorian rhinestone and millefiori frames, but they were photographs only of the living. Once in Vermont when I showed her a picture that I had dug up somewhere of her father as a young man, she hardly so much as glanced at it.

But there was one day, I remember, when in the midst of some conversation we were having about nothing in particular she suddenly turned to me and said out of the blue, "Do you really believe anything *happens* after you die?" and all at once she was present to me in a way she rarely was. She was no longer onstage. She was no longer in character. She had stepped off into the wings for a moment, and the words she had spoken were not in the script. Her face was for the moment not the one she had skillfully assembled in front of her dressing-table mirror that morning with lipstick, powder, and eyebrow pencil, but her own true face.

She had come a long way from the little girl in frilly white with the upside-down flowers in her lap. She was in her eighties with bad arthritis in her knees and was wearing whichever one of her many hearing aids she happened to have chosen that day, although none of them ever seemed to do her much good. I always suspected that it was not so much because she was deaf that she couldn't hear, but because there was so much she didn't want to hear that she chose to be deaf. To get anything through to her you had to say it at the top of your lungs, so in answer to her question, I said YES. I said I believed SOMETHING HAPPENS. But there are some things that cannot be shouted, and as soon as I tried in my more or less normal voice to tell her a little more about what I believed and why I believed it, I could see that she was not only not hearing, but also not listening. Just to have asked the question seemed for the time being to be as much as she could handle.

So later, when I got home, I tried to answer the question in a letter. I wrote her I believe that what happens when you die is that, in ways I knew no more about than she did, you are given back your life again, and I said that there were three reasons why I believed it. First, I wrote her, I believed it because, if I were God and loved the people I created and wanted them to become at last the best they had it in them to be, I couldn't imagine consigning them to oblivion when their time came with the job under the best of circumstance only a fraction done. Second, I said, I believed it, apart from any religious considerations, because I had a hunch it was true. I intuited it. I said that if the victims and the victimizers, the wise and the foolish, the good-hearted and the heartless all end up alike in the grave and that is the end of it, then life would be a black comedy, and to me, even at its worst, life doesn't *feel* like a black comedy. It feels like a mystery. It feels as though, at the innermost heart of it, there is Holiness, and that we experience all the horrors that go on both around us and within us *as* horrors rather than as just the way the cookie crumbles because, in our own innermost hearts, we belong to Holiness, which they are a tragic departure from. And lastly, I wrote her, I believe that what happens to us after we die is that we aren't dead forever because Jesus said so.

Buechner also writes about the end of his brother Jamie's life, and the prayer that he wrote for him to use as he passed away. It is a good prayer for all of us who want to trust a better story about our own lives, for those of us who want to join the eternal party.

One of our sons-in-law, David, was with him when he died a few hours later, and Jamie told him how he wished he knew how to thank him properly for all he had done, flying down from Boston four or five times those last few days to help him wind things up in every conceivable way. He said he wished he had some way to repay him for his inconceivable kindness, to which David replied that I had once said I might think about giving him the Uncle Wiggly books. "If I were you, I'd try to get that in writing," Jamie said, and those were among the last of all his words.

He never went to church except once in a while to hear me, and he didn't want a funeral, he told me—too much like a direct question, I suppose—but when I suggested maybe cocktails and dinner for some of his old friends in the fall when everybody got back to the city, he said that sounded like a good idea. But he did ask me if I would write a prayer for him that he could use, and David said that he had it there on the table beside him.

"Dear Lord, bring me through darkness into light. Bring me through pain into peace. Bring me through death into life. Be with me wherever I go, and with everyone I love. In Christ's name I ask it. Amen."

THE WIDE ROAD CALLED ORTHODOXY

SELECTIONS FROM HISTORIC CHRISTIAN TEACHERS ON LAST THINGS

Questions about eternal destinies have been on the minds of the believing community since the birth of the church. The testimony of the ages shows that matters relating to the end of all things, judgment, heaven, and hell have always been points of deliberation, disagreement, and mystery. The point of the following short excerpts is not to offer a unified case for a particular doctrine, but to reassure us and stimulate us to participate in the centuries-long conversation about the exciting new reality inaugurated by Jesus Christ.

God Is All in All

I am of opinion that the expression, by which God is said to be all in all, means that He is all in each individual person. Now He will be all in each individual in this way: when all which any rational understanding, cleansed from the dregs of every sort of vice, and with every cloud of wickedness completely swept away, can either feel, or understand, or think, will be wholly God; and when it will no longer behold or retain anything else than God, but when God will be the measure and standard of all its movements; and thus God will be all, for there will no longer be any distinction of good and evil, seeing evil nowhere exists; for God is all things, and to Him no evil is near: nor will there be any longer a desire to eat from the tree of the knowledge of good and evil, on the part of him who is always in the possession of good, and to whom God is all. So then, when the end has been restored to the beginning, and the termination of things compared with their commencement, that condition of things will be reestablished in which rational nature was placed, when it had no need to eat of the tree of the knowledge of good and evil; so that when all feeling of wickedness has been removed, and the individual has been purified and cleansed, He who alone is the one good God becomes to him all, and that not in the case of a few individuals, or of a considerable number, but He Himself is all in all. And when death shall no longer anywhere exist, nor the sting of death, nor any evil at all, then verily God will be all in all. . . .

Into this condition, then, we are to suppose that all this bodily substance of ours will be brought, when all things shall be reestablished in a state of unity, and when God shall be all in all. And this result must be understood as being brought about, not suddenly, but slowly and gradually, seeing that the process of amendment and correction will take place imperceptibly in the individual instances during the lapse of countless and unmeasured ages, some outstripping others, and tending by a swifter course towards perfection, while others again follow close at hand, and some again a long way behind; and thus, through the numerous and uncounted orders of progressive beings who are being reconciled to God from a state of enmity, the last enemy is finally reached, who is called death, so that he also may be destroyed, and no longer be an enemy. When, therefore, all rational souls shall have been restored to a condition of this kind, then the nature of this body of ours will undergo a change into the glory of a spiritual body.

—Origen, *De Prinicipiis*

We Can Set No Limits on the Agency of the Redeemer

If in this life there are so many ways for purification and repentance, how much more should there be after death! The purification of souls, when separated from the body, will be easier. We can set no limits to the agency of the Redeemer; to redeem, to rescue, to discipline, is his work, and so will he continue to operate after this life."

—Clement of Alexandria

Refined in a Furnace

Apocatastasis: A name given in the history of theology to the doctrine which teaches that a time will come when all free creatures will share in the grace of salvation; in a special way, the devils and lost souls. This doctrine was explicitly taught by St. Gregory of Nyssa, and in more than one passage. It first occurs in his *De anima et resurrectione* (P.G., XLVI, cols. 100, 101), where, in speaking of the punishment by fire assigned to souls after death, he compares it to the process whereby gold is refined in a furnace, through being separated from the dross with which it is alloyed. The punishment by fire is not, therefore, an end in itself, but is ameliorative; the very reason of its infliction is to separate the good from the evil in the soul. The process, moreover, is a painful one; the sharpness and duration of the pain are in proportion to the evil of which each soul is guilty; the flame lasts so long as there is any evil left to destroy. A time, then, will come, when all evil shall cease to be since it has no existence of its own apart from the free will, in which it inheres; when every free will shall be turned to God, shall be in God, and evil shall have no more wherein to exist. Thus, St. Gregory of Nyssa continues, shall the word of St. Paul be fulfilled: *Deus erit omnia in omnibus* ["God may be all in all"] (1 Cor. 15:28), which means that evil shall, ultimately, have an end, since, if God be all in all, there is no longer any place for evil.

—*The Catholic Encyclopedia*

God Himself Is Both Heaven and Hell

God himself is both heaven and hell, reward and punishment. All men have been created to see God unceasingly in His uncreated glory. Whether God will be for each man heaven or hell, reward or punishment, depends on man's response to God's love and on man's transformation from the state of selfish and self-centered love, to Godlike love which does not seek its own ends.

—John S. Romanides,
Franks, Romans,
Feudalism, and Doctrine

The Lost Are Annihilated, Not Tormented

The strong impression the Bible creates in this reader with regard to the fate of the finally impenitent wicked is a vivid sense of their final and irreversible destruction. The language and imagery used by Scripture is so powerful in this regard that it is remarkable more theologians have not picked up on it. The Bible repeatedly uses the language of death, destruction, ruin, and perishing when speaking of the fate of the wicked. It uses the imagery of fire consuming (not torturing) what is thrown into it. The images of fire and destruction together strongly suggest annihilation rather than unending torture. . . .

[Jesus] said that God could and perhaps would destroy body and soul in hell, if He must (Matt. 10:28). Jesus's words are reminiscent of John the Baptist's when he said that the wicked are like dry wood about to be thrown into the fire and like chaff to be burned in the unquenchable fire (Matt. 3:10, 12). He warned that the wicked will be cast away into hell like so much rejected garbage into the Gehenna of fire (Matt. 5:30), an allusion to the valley outside Jerusalem where sacrifices were once offered to Moloch (2 Kings 16:3; 21:6), and possibly the place where garbage actually smoldered and burned in Jesus's day. Our Lord said that the wicked will be burned up there just like weeds when thrown into the fire (Matt. 13:30, 42, 49, 50). The impression is a very strong one that the impenitent wicked can expect to be destroyed.

The apostle Paul communicates the same thing, plainly thinking of divine judgment as the destruction of the wicked. He writes of everlasting destruction which will come upon the wicked (2 Thess. 1:9). He warns that the wicked will reap corruption (Gal. 6:8). He states that God will destroy the wicked (1 Cor. 3:17; Phil. 1:28). He speaks of their fate as a death they deserve to die (Rom. 1:32) and which is the wages of their sins (Rom. 6:23). About the wicked, he states plainly and concisely: "Their end is destruction" (Phil. 3:19).

It is no different in the other New Testament books. Peter speaks of "the fire which has been kept until the day of judgment and the destruction of ungodly men" (2 Pet. 3:7). The author of the letter to the Hebrews speaks of the wicked who shrink back and are destroyed (Heb. 10:39). Peter says that false teachers who deny the Lord who bought them will bring upon themselves "swift destruction" (2 Pet. 2:1, 3). They will resemble the cities of Sodom and Gomorrah which were "condemned to extinction" (2 Pet. 2:6). They will perish like the ancient world perished when deluged in the great Flood (2 Pet. 3:6, 7). Jude also points to Sodom as an analogy to God's judgment, being the city which underwent "a punishment of eternal fire" (Jude 7). Similarly, the Apocalypse of John speaks of the lake of fire consuming the wicked and of the second death (Rev. 20:14, 15).

At the very least it should be obvious to any impartial reader that the Bible may legitimately be read to teach the final destruction of the wicked without difficulty. I am not making it up. It is not wishful thinking. It is simply a natural interpretation of Scripture on the subject of divine judgment. I think it is outrageous for traditionalists to say that a biblical basis for the destruction of the wicked is lacking. What is in short supply are texts supporting the traditional view.

—Clark Pinnock,
"The Destruction of the
Finally Impenitent"

Hell as Cure for an Illness

Paradise and Hell exist not in the form of a threat and a punishment on the part of God but in the form of an illness and a cure. Those who are cured and those who are purified experience the illuminating energy of divine grace, while the uncured and ill experience the caustic energy of God.

—Metropolitan Hierotheos
of Nafpaktos,
Life After Death

No Person Can Pass Judgment

No man, even though he has the gifts of the Spirit, can pass judgment on peoples of this world who still struggle on without your grace.

—Augustine, *Confessions*

Justice and Mercy Are One and the Same

I believe that justice and mercy are simply one and the same thing; without justice to the full there can be no mercy, and without mercy to the full there can be no justice; that such is the mercy of God that he will hold his children in the consuming fire of his distance until they pay the uttermost farthing, until they drop the purse of selfishness with all the dross that is in it, and rush home to the Father and the Son, and the many brethren rush inside the centre of the life-giving fire whose outer circles burn. I believe that no hell will be lacking which would help the just mercy of God to redeem his children.

—George MacDonald,
The Unspoken Sermons

All Justice and Mercy Will Be Done

On the heathen, see Tim. 4:10. Also in Matt. 25:31–46 the people don't sound as if they were believers. Also the doctrine of Christ's descending into Hell (i.e., Hades, the land of the dead; not Gehenna the land of the lost) and preaching to the dead; and that would be outside time and would include those who died long after Him as well as those who died before He was born as Man. I don't think we know the details; we must just stick to the view that (a) all justice and mercy will be done, (b) but nevertheless it is our duty to do all we can to convert unbelievers.

—C. S. Lewis,
The Collected Letters of C. S. Lewis

Hell Is Locked from the Inside

I willingly believe that the damned are, in one sense, successful, rebels to the end; that the doors of hell are locked on the *inside.*

—C. S. Lewis,
The Problem of Pain

All That Are in Hell, Choose It

There are only two kinds of people in the end: those who say to God, "Thy will be done," and those to whom God says, in the end, "*Thy* will be done." All that are in Hell, choose it. Without that self-choice there could be no Hell. No soul that seriously and constantly desires joy will ever miss it. Those who seek find. To those who knock it is opened.

—C. S. Lewis,
The Great Divorce

God Is Faithful

There are two realities to which you must cling. First, God has promised that you will receive the love you have been searching for. And second, God is faithful to that promise.

—Henri Nouwen,
The Inner Voice of Love

Sanctifying Ordinary Lives

Jesus lived the ordinary life of the men of his time, in order to sanctify the ordinary lives of men of all time.

—Thomas Merton,
Thoughts on Solitude

The Triumph of God

I believe implicitly in the ultimate and complete triumph of God, the time when all things will be subject to him, and when God will be everything to everyone (1 Cor. 15:24–28). For me this has certain consequences. If one man remains outside the love of God at the end of time, it means that that one man has defeated the love of God—and that is impossible. Further, there is only one way in which we can think of the triumph of God. If God was no more than a King or Judge, then it would be possible to speak of his triumph, if his enemies were agonizing in hell or were totally and completely obliterated and wiped out. But God is not only King and Judge; God is *Father*—he is indeed Father more than anything else. No father could be happy while there were members of his family forever in agony. No father would count it a triumph to obliterate the disobedient members of his family. The only triumph a father can know is to have all his family back home. The only victory love can enjoy is the day when its offer of love is answered by the return of love. The only possible final triumph is a universe loved by and in love with God.

—William Barclay,
A Spiritual Autobiography

Universal Reconciliation

There is no good reason why we should forbid ourselves, or be forbidden, openness to the possibility that in the reality of God and man in Jesus Christ there is contained . . . the supremely unexpected withdrawal of the final threat. . . . If for a moment we accept the unfalsified truth of the reality which even now so forcefully limits the perverted human situation, does it not point plainly in the direction of a truly eternal divine patience and deliverance of a . . . universal reconciliation? If we are forbidden to count on this . . . we are surely commanded the more definitely to hope and pray for this.

—Karl Barth,
Church Dogmatics

Q&A WITH ROB BELL

AN INTERVIEW BY DAVID VANDERVEEN

With the Companion *guide to* Love Wins *coming out, I'd love to ask you a few questions about writing the book, traveling, and your reflections now that the book has been out for half a year. Is there any one event or experience that stands out for you?*

Yes, there is. Or maybe I should say, yes, there are. I just received a letter from a young woman who has been suicidal for years now; she wrote me to say that since she was exposed in the book to the idea that God is love, she hasn't wanted to kill herself. She went on to say that the dark, menacing images of God she had been carrying around for years had etched themselves on her psyche and essentially convinced her that if that's who's running the world, why go on living?

And you've gotten other letters like this?

Yep. My experience has been that an untold number of people were introduced somewhere along the way to a God who is not good. And so they want to believe, they want meaning and purpose and relationship, and they're deeply moved by Jesus, but the God behind it all is fundamentally suspect for them. They just can't do it. And when they're given a glimpse of the God I believe Jesus came to show us, they come alive. It's extraordinary to see.

Wow.

Yes, "wow" is one of the words I use often. For me, theology is not an abstract exercise. It's about the search for words and language to describe how real people navigate a real world and find the divine in the midst of it all.

Say more about that.

Sure. I'll start with an example. At a number of the Q&A sessions I did surrounding the release of the book, people wanted to talk about *orthodoxy.* This word comes from two words: the word "ortho," which means "correct," and the word "doxy," which comes from the word "think, or apprehend." So to be orthodox is to think correctly about something or, in the case of religion, somebody. And it's important, very important. What we think and believe deeply shapes us and how we live and move and have our being in the world.

But it wasn't Jesus's point. He talked about how we actually live. He said the greatest command was to love

God and love our neighbor. He talked about what is called "orthopraxy"—"praxy" meaning "practice." Correct practice, conduct, living. What's happened for a number of people in our world is that orthodoxy and orthopraxy got separated, and so massive discussions have gone on about orthodoxy without anyone saying, "Excuse me, but you need two legs to walk."

So what I hear you saying is that ideas have consequences.

Exactly, and that means it's very important that we don't separate thinking from living. It's a holistic reality, an integrated life, that Jesus calls us to.

Now I'd like to get your take on a few big issues. First, how do you respond when people want you to talk about God's wrath and anger?

Good question. I answer with a question: "What kind of mountain have we come to?"

Usually people then ask me, "Huh? What kind of mountain?"

And I say, "Yes, what kind of mountain?" Because the writer of Hebrews says that we have not come to a mountain that is burning with fire and darkness and gloom and storm, a mountain that is so terrifying that Moses trembled with fear. The writer says we've come to a different mountain, to the city of the living God, where there are thousands and thousands of angels in joyful assembly, where Jesus has reversed the heartache and despair that's been present since the first humans suffered. It's a stunning picture, an epic metaphor if there ever was one!

Hebrews presents us with two mountains, two pictures, two realities, and essentially shouts: "Jesus has changed everything! We're not at that mountain anymore; we've come to a new place, a place of worship and gratitude." That's the place that compels me, that's the vision that captures my heart.

Going along with that, then, can you say more about the cross? How do the two mountains relate to the cross?

In a big way. The driving question, then, is this: Was Jesus's death on the cross enough? Was it sufficient? Did it pay whatever price needed to be paid, did it meet whatever criteria needed to be met? Did it, in essence, do the job? And I believe that the resounding, joyous, exuberant declaration of the New Testament is that Jesus has taken care of everything that needed to be taken care of. I realize that's not very technical or scholarly language, but that's my point. We can trust Jesus.

It truly is finished. This is why it's so lethal to thriving faith when people talk as though perhaps it isn't finished. Or that Jesus's death and resurrection weren't enough.

A question that haunts a number of people who have read your book is the whole idea of a second chance to "get right with God" after you die. Does this idea that there may be more chances mean that it doesn't matter how you live now, you can always fix things later?

Absolutely not. Unequivocally no. And here's why. Do you have a backyard?

Excuse me?

Do you have a backyard?

Well, yes, I have a backyard.

Good. Then if I told you that there is a million dollars buried in your backyard, would you finish this interview, and then maybe go to eat somewhere, maybe then stop by the hardware store and perhaps do a few other errands, maybe then get a drink with a friend? No! You'd be out of here in a second. You'd race home and grab a shovel.

This new awareness of a gift that is already in your possession would create within you a profound sense of urgency, a pressing belief that your actions mattered in a whole new way. And what does Jesus say as he comes marching through the Galilee? Repent! It's an invigorating, enlivening call to do something with your life, to wake up, to see the God who is all around us all the time. The one thing the gospel is not is a call to passivity, to check out until a later date when things are supposed to then get exciting.

And I assume this relates, then, to the ways you talk about hell.

Definitely. If people believe in Jesus because they don't want to go somewhere bad, what kind of love relationship is that? I didn't marry my wife because I didn't want to be with some other woman; I married her because I couldn't imagine the rest of my life without her.

So the gospel is a positive?

Well, yes, it's a positive, but it's much more significant than that. It's about who God is and what it means to live in constant conscious contact with God, to be connected to the ground of your being. When people say that if you take away the threat of punishment, then no one will have any motivation to believe in Jesus, they are in that very moment degrading Jesus. They're saying something incredibly derogatory about Jesus, that the best he offers is an escape. They're revealing a seriously bankrupt, empty gospel that doesn't have much in the way of anything good, just promises that you'll avoid something bad. Jesus comes to us now to offer us the eternal life of God now, so that we'll experience joy and peace and healing now.

You raise a lot of questions in the book, and then you give a lot of answers, and then you ask a lot more questions. Do you ever see yourself running out of questions?

What do you think?

CONTRIBUTORS

Pope Benedict XVI, previously known as Cardinal Joseph Ratzinger, is the German-born Bishop of Rome and pontiff for the worldwide Catholic Church. He is a scholar and author of numerous books, including two volumes so far in his Jesus of Nazareth series.

Frederick Buechner, an ordained Presbyterian minister who has been hailed by the *Boston Globe* as "one of our finest writers," is the author of thirty works of fiction and nonfiction. His work has been nominated for the Pulitzer Prize (*Godric*) and the National Book Award (*Lion Country,* now collected in *The Book of Bebb*), and he has been honored by the American Academy and Institute of Arts and Letters. He divides his time between Vermont and Florida.

Oswald J. Chambers was a prominent early twentieth-century Scottish Protestant Christian minister and teacher, best known as the author of the widely read devotional *My Utmost for His Highest*.

David Dark, the critically acclaimed author of *The Sacredness of Questioning Everything, Everyday Apocalypse,* and *The Gospel According to America,* is an educator who recently completed his Ph.D. in Religious Studies at Vanderbilt University. He has had articles published in *Paste, Oxford American, Books and Culture,* and *Christian Century,* among others. A frequent speaker, Dark has also appeared on C-SPAN's Book-TV and in an award-winning documentary, *Marketing the Message.* He lives with his singer-songwriter wife, Sarah Masen, and their three children in Nashville.

Cathleen Falsani is a journalist, author, and blogger. She is an award-winning religion columnist who writes for Religion News Service and *Sojourners* magazine. From 2000 to 2010 she was the religion writer for the *Chicago Sun-Times*. Falsani is the author of several books, including *The God Factor, Sin Boldly, The Dude Abides,* and, most recently, *Belieber.* She lives with her husband and son in Laguna Beach, California.

Jack Heaslip is a true Irish sage. He hails from just north of Dublin, Ireland, and writes with the certainty of a man who talks with God. An ordained Anglican clergyman, for the last fifteen years Jack has been the spiritual adviser for the band U2, traveling all over the world with Bono, the Edge, Larry, and Adam, ministering to the band and their small city of five hundred crew members who build the sets, hang the lights, move girders, construct the huge Claw for the 360 tour, and help put the show on for over seven million fans around the world.

Anne Lamott is the author of the *New York Times* bestsellers *Grace (Eventually), Plan B, Traveling Mercies,* and *Operating Instructions* as well as seven novels, including *Rosie* and *Crooked Little Heart*. She is a past recipient of a Guggenheim Fellowship.

Clayton Libolt, Ph.D., is pastor at River Terrace Christian Reformed Church, Lansing, Michigan.

Donald Miller is a bestselling author and public speaker based in Portland, Oregon. His books include *A Million Miles in a Thousand Years, Searching for God Knows What, Blue Like Jazz, To Own a Dragon,* and *Through Painted Deserts.*

Shayne Moore, M.A., is the author of *Global Soccer Mom: Changing the World Is Easier Than You Think*. In addition to being an author, she is a speaker, mama of three, and outspoken advocate in the fight against extreme poverty and global AIDS. Moore is one of the original members of the ONE Campaign, The Campaign to Make Poverty History (www.one.org). Moore sits on the executive board of directors for Upendo Village, an HIV/AIDS clinic in Kenya, and on the board of directors for Growers First, which empowers rural farmers in the developing world. Moore has written for ONE's blog and *Christianity Today*'s Gifted for Leadership and pens a column in the magazine *FullFill.* Check out her personal blog at www.GlobalSoccerMom.com.

Richard J. Mouw is president of Fuller Theological Seminary in Pasadena, California, and the author of many books, including *Uncommon Decency*. His blog can be found at netbloghost.com/mouw/.

Glenn Parrish is a professional in social and venture philanthropy with a background in youth ministry. He is a board member with Sacred Harvest Foundation and is a founding partner in the for-profit Growers First Coffee company as well as an adviser to the Growers First Foundation.

Peter Rollins is the author of *How (Not) to Speak of God, The Fidelity of Betrayal, The Orthodox Heretic and Other Impossible Tales,* and *Insurrection.* A popular lecturer and storyteller, he is the founder of ikon, a faith group that has gained an international reputation for blending live music, visual imagery, soundscapes, theater, ritual, and reflection. Rollins received his higher education at Queens University, Belfast, where he earned degrees (with distinction) in Scholastic Philosophy (B.A. Hons.), Political Theory (M.A.), and Post-Structural Religious Philosophy (Ph.D.). He is currently a research associate with the Irish School of Ecumenics at Trinity College, Dublin. He was born in Belfast, Northern Ireland, but currently resides in Greenwich, Connecticut.

N. T. Wright is the former Bishop of Durham in the Church of England and one of the world's leading Bible scholars. He is now serving as the Chair of New Testament and Early Christianity at University of St. Andrews's School of Divinity. For twenty years he taught New Testament studies at Cambridge, McGill, and Oxford Universities, and he has been featured on ABC News, "Dateline NBC," and "Fresh Air." Wright is the award-winning author of *Simply Jesus, After You Believe, Surprised by Hope, Simply Christian,* and *Scripture and the Authority of God,* as well as the much heralded series Christian Origins and the Question of God.

Rob Bell is the founding pastor of Mars Hill Bible Church in Grand Rapids, Michigan. He is the author of the *New York Times* bestselling *Love Wins, Velvet Elvis, Sex God, Jesus Wants to Save Christians,* and *Drops Like Stars.* A graduate of Wheaton College and Fuller Theological Seminary, Bell speaks to sold-out crowds across the world and appeared in a pioneering series of short films called NOOMA. He and his wife, Kristen, have three children. Visit the author online at www.robbell.com.

David Vanderveen is the former managing editor of the *Mars Hill Review,* founding publisher of *Krakoosh Magazine,* and is a regular columnist for *The Laguna Beach Independent.* Raised in Western Michigan, David received his undergraduate college education at Wheaton and Calvin Colleges in philosophy and political science. He has been interviewed and featured in *AdWeek, BeverageWorld, NewsWeek, Centered Magazine, Laguna Beach Magazine, The OC Weekly,* and other publications. David has a longtime commitment to social issues politically, ideologically, religiously. He has served as the director of public relations at the Acton Institute for the Study of Religion and Liberty and executive director of Americans for Limited Terms, a nonprofit organization. David is married to his wife of eighteen years, Sarah, has two sons, and lives in Laguna Beach, California.

PERMISSIONS

“Questioning God,” by David Dark, from *The Sacredness of Questioning Everything,* pp. 14–19. © Copyright 2009 by David Dark. Used by permission of Zondervan.

“The Temptation of Religious Success,” by Oswald Chambers, from *My Utmost for His Highest,* for April 22. © Copyright 1935, 1963 by Oswald Chambers Publications Assn., Ltd. Used by permission of Discovery House Publishers, Box 3566, Grand Rapids, MI 49501. All rights reserved.

“Going to Heaven?” by N. T. Wright, from *How God Became King: The Forgotten Story of the Gospels,* chapter 2. © Copyright 2012 by Nicholas Thomas Wright. Used by permission of HarperOne, an imprint of HarperCollins Publishers.

“Hell on Earth,” by Shayne Moore, from *Global Soccer Mom: Changing the World Is Easier Than You Think,* chapter 9: "A Hope-Shaped Ache." © Copyright 2011 by Shayne Moore. Used by permission of Zondervan.

"The Secret," by Peter Rollins, from *How (Not) to Speak of God.* © Copyright 2006 by Peter Rollins. Used by permission of Paraclete Press.

"What Is Eternal Life?" by Pope Benedict XVI from *Spe Salvi,* Encyclical Letter of the Supreme Pontiff Benedict XVI to the Bishops, Priests, and Deacons, Men and Women Religious, and All the Lay Faithful, On Christian Hope, November 30, 2007.

"Stingy Orthodoxy or Generous Orthodoxy," by Richard J. Mouw, from "The Orthodoxy of Rob Bell," Mouw's Musings blog, March 15, 2011 (http://www.netbloghost.com/mouw/?p=188). Used by permission.

"Confession," by Donald Miller, from *Blue Like Jazz: Nonreligious Thoughts on Christian Spirituality,* pp. 121–25. © Copyright 2003 by Donald Miller. Used by permission of Thomas Nelson Publishers.

"All Right. You Can Come In," by Anne Lamott, from *Traveling Mercies: Some Thoughts on Faith,* pp. 48–50. © Copyright 1999 by Anne Lamott. Used by permission of Anchor Books, a division of Random House.

"Do You Really Believe Anything *Happens* After You Die?" by Frederick Buechner, from *The Eyes of the Heart: A Memoir of the Lost and Found,* pp. 14–16, 162–63. © Copyright 1999 by Frederick Buechner. Used by permission of HarperOne, an imprint of HarperCollins Publishers.